Tiger

ALSO BY JOHN STREGE

Off the Record

a biography of

Tiger Woods

JOHN STREGE
BROADWAY BOOKS   NEW YORK

BROADWAY

TIGER: A BIOGRAPHY OF TIGER WOODS. Copyright © 1997 by John
Strege. All rights reserved. Printed in the United States of America. No part of
this book may be reproduced or transmitted in any form or by any means,
electronic or mechanical, including photocopying, recording, or by any
information storage and retrieval system, without written permission from the
publisher. For information, address Broadway Books, a division of Bantam
Doubleday Dell Publishing Group, Inc., 1540 Broadway, New York, NY 10036.

Broadway Books titles may be purchased for business or promotional use or for
special sales. For information, please write to: Special Markets Department,
Bantam Doubleday Dell Publishing Group, Inc., 1540 Broadway, New York, NY
10036.

BROADWAY BOOKS and its logo, a letter B bisected on the diagonal, are
trademarks of Broadway Books, a division of Bantam Doubleday Dell Publishing
Group, Inc.

Library of Congress Cataloging-in-Publication Data

Strege, John.
    Tiger : a biography of Tiger Woods / by John Strege. — 1st ed.
      p. cm.
    ISBN 0-553-06219-0 (hc)
    1. Woods, Tiger. 2. Golfers—United States—Biography.
I. Title.
GV964.W66S87   1997
796.352'092—dc21
  [B]   97-9057
                                      CIP

Designed by Bonni Leon-Berman

97 98 99 00 01 10 9 8 7

FOR MARLENE,
WITH LOVE AND ADMIRATION

contents

The doormat on the front porch of the Woodses' home in Cypress, California, said, "Duffers Welcome," which I interpreted to mean me. And so I stepped across their threshold and into their lives and was graciously given the best seat in the house to watch one of sport's most fascinating stories unfold.

I wish to express my appreciation to Tiger for permitting me to witness his development as a golfer and as a person from a unique perspective. Over the years, he has been generous with his time and unfailingly polite, and I have treasured this opportunity.

I am indebted to his parents, Earl and Kultida Woods, who are rightfully proud of their son and their role in his success. When you write about fourteen-year-old athletes, even those as bright as Tiger, they are seldom useful sources of information. As a result, you tend to lean on the parents, who become invaluable resources, as was the case here. From a professional relationship a friendship evolved with Earl and Kultida, and I have cherished that more than they know.

I owe a debt of gratitude that can never be repaid to Larry Dorman, the esteemed golf writer for the *New York Times*, without whose help this project would not have been possible. I am proud to call him my friend. I would also like to thank another friend, Jaime Diaz, for his unending support over the years. For my money, Diaz and Dorman are the two best golf writers in America.

My agent, Freya Manston, is a persistent woman who made no promises but responded as though she had. She is a remarkable woman and a friend, and her tireless efforts on my behalf will never be forgotten.

Of incalculable help was Dave Strege, an accomplished journalist and a preeminent outdoors writer. Thanks also to his wonderful wife, Cindy, for permitting me to borrow him.

acknowledgments

ACKNOWLEDGMENTS

Special thanks to Rudy Duran, the golf pro responsible for pointing a four-year-old Tiger in the right direction. My appreciation for his selfless contributions to this project is limitless. Thanks also to Jay Brunza, an officer and a gentleman; to Butch Harmon, a pro's pro and the best teacher in the game; and to John Merchant, whose role in and passion for advancing minority participation in golf should not be overlooked.

For all those who shared their recollections—notably Don Crosby, Mike Kruse, Wally Goodwin, Conrad Ray, Jake Poe, Eri Crum, and Tom Sargent—you have my deepest appreciation.

Thanks to my colleagues in the press tent for their contributions to, and/or support of, this book, notably Mark Soltau, Paul Lester, Robinson Holloway, T. R. Reinman, John Marvel, Lee Patterson, Wes Seeley, and Mark Mitchell.

I would be remiss in failing to acknowledge those most important to me; their enthusiasm and encouragement was of inestimable help. They include, first and foremost, my mother and father, Dorothy and Bill Strege, as well as Liz and Bill Spencer, Teresa and Leonard Strege, Trina and Howard Miller, Lorraine Allred, Craig Hoelzel, Harry Hoelzel, and Dorothy and Bob Mericle. Thanks also to Debbie Johnson for her assistance.

Chuck Scott has provided counsel and friendship and Steve Bisheff has been a mentor and a friend, and I am grateful to both. Thanks as well to Tom Bonk for his friendship and moral support through a sometimes hectic and difficult time and to Robert Barth and Joy Gibney.

My indefatigable editor at Broadway Books, Suzanne Oaks, as friendly as she is skillful, kept this project on track without once losing patience with me. It was a privilege to have had the opportunity to work with her. I am grateful also to her assistant, Ann Campbell, for her help and timely words of encouragement. Finally, my heartfelt appreciation to William Shinker, the publisher of Broadway Books, for providing me with this opportunity.

Tiger

An eerie quiet descended over the valley, a lush landscape of farmland and pine trees through which two golf courses had been built near the Sunset Highway twenty miles west of Portland, Oregon. It was so quiet you could hear a putt drop, if one was inclined to drop—a remote possibility given the factors conspiring against the putt in question.

It might have measured thirty feet had it not been attached to the rack and stretched by the pressure of the situation, the thirty-fifth hole of the final match of the ninety-sixth United States Amateur Championship. Thirty feet or thirty miles, the distance represented a journey across time, ninety-six years of reel reduced to this, a single frame frozen in the mind's eye: Tiger Woods putting, his quest for a historic and unprecedented third consecutive U.S. Amateur championship hanging in the balance.

This was potentially another in a series of defining moments in the career of Tiger Woods, the kind that compels him to elevate his game—ostensibly by the sheer force of his will—to meet the enormity of a task. Jay Brunza, his longtime sports psychologist, compares Woods's innate ability to make crucial putts to that of Nicklaus. "They both seem to will the ball into the hole," he said.

The crowd on the Witch Hollow Course had grown to more than fifteen thousand, the largest to witness a U.S. Amateur final since Bobby Jones pursued the Grand Slam at Merion in 1930. The people were entranced by the precocious and seemingly indomitable Woods, a rare multiethnic presence in a game with eighteen greens, but noticeably fewer blacks. They had put down their money to see him apply the final flourish to his amateur legacy, and they watched in stunned disbelief as he displayed an unsteady hand and, at the midway point of the thirty-six-hole match, fell behind to Steve Scott by five holes.

At the lunch break, Scott and his caddie and girlfriend, Kristi

Hommel, retreated to the merchandise tent, presumably in search of a bag in which to hold the lead before it slipped from his grasp. Scott knew well that many others had let one slip away to this young man who was so efficient at fending off defeat.

"He was five down and yet I would have bet my life that he was going to win it, although I had no idea how he could," said Woods's Stanford teammate, Jake Poe, watching at home in Columbia, Missouri.

That golf is not a life-or-death affair is a concept that has always eluded Woods. His approach to a match, particularly a match of historic significance, is that of a man who equates a loss with a mortal wound. When threatened with defeat, he will fight as though struggling for his life.

The wreckage of those who once had Woods down and then let him up lies scattered across the pages of golf history. He is one of only three to have ever won United States Golf Association events in five consecutive years. To do so he made battle casualties of Trip Kuehne—who had Woods down six holes early in the final of the 1994 U.S. Amateur and lost at the thirty-sixth hole, and Ryan Armour—who was 2 up with two holes to play and lost on the first extra hole in the final of the 1993 U.S. Junior Amateur.

Steve Scott, a golfer from the University of Florida, built what would have been a safe lead in other matches, but he knew better than to begin crafting a victory speech now. "That's not good enough," he said of a five-hole lead. "Just keep playing, because there're so many holes. I've seen what he's done in the past, and I won't be happy until I have him 10 up or something. He's that tough."

When Woods began to claw his way back into the match, Scott was not surprised. Early in the afternoon round, Woods won the third, fourth, and fifth holes, then made an eleven-foot putt at nine to reduce the deficit to a single hole. On the par-3 tenth hole, 194 yards, Scott put his tee shot into the heavy rough beyond the green, leaving him with a delicate, downhill, borderline-impossible chip, with the lead he had enjoyed since early morning suddenly endangered. He landed the ball softly on the downslope, but it gained speed on its journey toward the hole, and in a fortuitous turn for Scott, it banged against the stick and fell into the cup. This birdie might have shattered the resolve of a lesser foe than Tiger.

But even when Scott made a birdie again on the eleventh hole, Woods trumped it by holing a difficult thirty-four-foot eagle putt with three feet of break. "I thought I could build a little momentum and he just killed it with that eagle," Scott recounted afterward. "Just killed it. I thought I was going to keep going and he killed the momentum."

Even though Scott won the fourteenth hole with a birdie to reopen his two-hole lead, he held this dangerously close margin only until the two arrived at the thirty-fourth hole of the match. Tiger had been struggling with his putter and had missed a ten-foot birdie putt moments earlier. But on this one he mobilized his ability to hole putts when it is imperative that he do so, and he made an eight-footer for birdie to pull within one, stoking the wildfire of a drama that was already burning out of control.

Minutes later, they stood on the green at the thirty-fifth hole, the par-4 seventeenth, and Woods had thirty feet to tie the match. The golf world was watching, breathlessly waiting to see whether a legend that defied conventional definition was capable of expanding.

A tournament that once garnered scant network television interest had suddenly evolved into must-see TV, the Amateur hours, on NBC. PGA Tour players in the locker room at the Greater Vancouver Open watched, spellbound. Viewers at home had abandoned the World Series of Golf on CBS, airing opposite the Amateur and turned to NBC instead. The World Series featured a quality international field that included Greg Norman and Phil Mickelson vying for the title, but the U.S. Amateur, with its mounting drama and Tiger Woods's quest for making golf history, prevailed.

The public was mesmerized by Woods. He was twenty, a junior-to-be at Stanford, and he had moved to the fore in golf—the first amateur to do so since Bobby Jones, who had retired without turning professional. The subplot of the tournament was whether Tiger was writing the denouement to his amateur career; speculation was rampant that he intended to make his professional debut the following week at the Greater Milwaukee Open. Nike was rumored to be a suitor enticing him with a multimillion dollar contract offer. And Phil Knight, the company CEO, was a conspicuous component of Tiger's gallery the entire week. Another rumor had the Nike corporate jet standing by at the Hillsborough Airport, ready to whisk the whole Woods family off to Milwaukee just hours after the Amateur concluded.

Tiger, meanwhile, was concerned, not with negotiating contracts, but with negotiating a difficult thirty-foot putt that imperiled his historical journey. He carefully read the break, then visualized the putt in his mind. He concluded that this was not a difficult putt for him; it would break five inches and funnel toward the hole, and on this shot speed was not that important. No matter how hard he hit it, it would still break five inches.

He took his three practice strokes, a part of his usual preputt routine, and then addressed the ball. He looked at the hole once, twice, then drew the club back. As though guided by a divine hand, Woods's putt, calibrated to break five inches, broke neither more nor less, and the ball dove into the hole, igniting from the crowd a thunderous ovation that reverberated across the valley and throughout the golf world. Scott heard none of it, his senses numbed by what he had just witnessed, a brush-stroke of genius by a virtuoso. "Unbelievable," he murmured. There was nothing more to say.

Woods began punching the air with his trademark upper-cut—a knockout punch in fact—one he reserved for those moments when he had an opponent on the ropes. Once again he had stared down defeat, in this case a five-hole deficit. He had squared the match against long odds, odds that failed to account for the fortitude of a young man who had long ago established that he was never really a longshot.

For Woods, victory was again imminent, and he knew it, even as those watching struggled to believe it. In a resounding way, Tiger had put the golf world on notice. It had better brace itself because the future had arrived and the assault had begun.

chapter one

Lieutenant Colonel Earl Woods was not oblivious, certainly, to impending danger. It was his second tour of duty in Vietnam, and he was keenly aware that war indiscriminately claims its victims. Hit-and-run guerrillas preyed on anyone who failed to keep an eye trained to the rear, but even the most careful were susceptible to stopping a sniper's bullet. A former Green Beret, Woods had learned that the enemy could be anywhere, perhaps everywhere, and so it was with seasoned caution that he proceeded along a rice-paddy dike.

The uneasy calm that periodically pervades a war when the guns are quiet—always a temporary state in Vietnam—had settled over the valley. The tranquillity was suddenly pierced by a shriek.

"Get down, Woody!" a voice yelled.

Woods dove for cover a moment before a sniper's bullets riddled the space he had vacated; it was a call too close for comfort. The warning was the work of Nguyen Phong, a lieutenant colonel, Woods's South Vietnamese army counterpart. He had saved Woods's life.

A short time later, well beyond the range of the sniper, the troops stopped to rest. His heart rate again normal, Woods curled up in a thicket of bamboo to take a much needed nap. Just as he dozed off, Phong's yelling suddenly woke him.

"Don't move, Woody!" Phong said. "There's a bamboo viper about two inches from your right eye."

Woods rolled his eyes to the right and stared into the mouth of a venomous snake. His heart was pounding the staccato drumbeat of a man paralyzed by fear, fortunately so, since his survival depended on absolute stillness. Eventually the snake lost interest and withdrew, and Woods bolted from the thicket. In the span of about twenty minutes Phong had saved his life twice.

Woods was there in an advisory capacity to Phong and the South Vietnamese army, and he earned a Vietnamese Silver Star for his role in a mission conducted in a Vietcong-occupied village through which Phong had led him. It was here among the rice paddies and in the jungles and villages of Vietnam that the first name in golf had its genesis.

"He was special," Earl said of his friend, to whom he now owed his life. "He was good in combat. He was a tiger in combat, so I began calling him 'Tiger.'" But after Earl returned home and Vietnam fell two years later, he never heard from Phong again.

Woods never forgot his colleague and friend and, as a tribute to him and a means by which to keep his memory alive, he vowed that if he was ever blessed with another son he would call him Tiger. Woods already had two sons and a daughter, he was approaching forty, and the likelihood of his fathering another child seemed remote to him. Over time and because of the long distances required by his overseas military commitments, he and his wife grew apart, and they divorced a few months before the U.S. Army dispatched Woods to Bangkok.

While stationed there, he met a pretty young Thai woman named Kultida, or Tida, as her family and friends called her, who was employed as a secretary in the Army office.

Immediately attracted, Earl asked her on a date and they agreed to meet at eight. But he was under the impression it was eight that night, while she thought it was eight the following morning. "Thai girls not go out at night," she said. That night, Earl waited patiently, then impatiently, until it was apparent she was not going to show. He was convinced he had been stood up. The following morning, when Earl failed to show, Kultida was sure she had been stood up. A proud, defiant woman who does not take rejection lightly, she and a friend went on a manhunt. When she found Earl, she said tersely, "We had a date."

"Yeah, last night," Earl said.

"We still have date," she insisted. It was a holy day in Bangkok and she asked that he take her to the Temple of the Reclining Buddha. Earl knew that he had met his match in will. "So I took her to the church," Earl said.

Their relationship flourished and Woods brought her back to the States, to Brooklyn, where they were married in 1969. Six years later, with Kultida pregnant, they were shopping for a house in Orange County, California, near the McDonnell Douglas plant where Earl had taken a job as a contracts administrator upon his retirement from the military. A particular neighborhood in Cypress appealed to them—a quiet block of relatively new homes, with a small park around the corner and an elementary school two blocks away.

A real estate agent attempted to warn them away. They would not be comfortable here, the agent said—code for "white neighborhood." But Earl refused to be intimidated. The neighborhood was well kept and the homes affordable and close to Earl's work, so against the agent's advice, they bought a modest two-bedroom tract house on a corner lot.

Earl and Kultida put out a welcome mat, but the neighbors hardly reciprocated. The Woods home became a target of open bigotry, driven in part by the then widely accepted belief that property values declined in neighborhoods when black families moved in. Their housewarming gifts were windfall limes from neighborhood trees delivered as fastballs and aimed at windows. In a matter of weeks, arms throwing limes gave way to guns shooting BBs, an escalation in hostilities that might have made other families start packing. The Green Beret was not inclined to retreat, however. The Woodses stood their ground, and when it became apparent that they intended to stay, a cease-fire emerged.

The new baby boy Earl had thought he might never have arrived on December 30, 1975. Kultida chose to call him Eldrick, a name she devised by using the first letters of the parents' first names. Even though Earl reluctantly acquiesced to the name, he still intended to deliver on his vow to honor Nguyen Phong, his Vietnamese friend. From the cradle, Eldrick Woods was called Tiger.

Tiger did not emerge from the womb displaying a Nike swoosh. The nature of the gift that had been delivered to the Woods household was not immediately evident. It took several months. It was not that the baby suddenly stood in his crib and expertly coiled his torso, his shoulders perpendicular to the target, his left arm straight. Or that he plumb-bobbed his rattle. But it may have been the way little Tiger was mesmerized by his father's golf swing, his eyes tracing the path of the club and the sound made by the thwack of clubface against ball, a symphony to the baby's ears. Or it may have been the sawed-off putter he toted around the house. Whatever it was, Earl Woods understood early on that genius had arrived in his midst and that it was wearing diapers. He later said he knew what kind of golfer he would be before Tiger was even one.

Earl had taken up golf only a year earlier, when he succumbed to the constant pestering of a fellow Army officer. Once a catcher at Kansas State University, Earl considered himself a capable athlete and was embarrassed when he was so thoroughly beaten at a game in which the ball was a stationary target. He was leaving the Army in a few months, and he made it his mission to defeat his friend before returning to civilian life. He began working tirelessly on his golf, spending hours a day at the base driving range. He then challenged his friend to a rematch. Earl shot 81 and won by 4.

"I got hooked on golf in that round," Woods said. "I realized what I'd been missing my whole life. I decided if I had another son, I'd introduce him to golf early on."

His translation of "early on" was six months old. Aggressively working on his own game, he reduced his handicap to three with the help of a makeshift driving range he had constructed in his garage using a piece of carpet and a net. While he beat balls into the net with a 5-iron, he stationed the baby's highchair in the garage where Tiger sat quietly and watched, enchanted by this curious activity. When Kultida came in to feed him, she was an unwelcome distraction to the baby, who stubbornly resisted her attempts to interrupt him. Eventually they reached a compromise. Earl would hit a shot, then Tiger would receive a spoonful of food. They repeated this until Tiger was fed; he never tired of watching his father swing the club.

One day when Tiger was nine months old, Earl sat down to rest and his son climbed from the highchair, hoisted a club Earl had cut down for him, and put a ball in place. He waggled his club once, looked at his target, waggled the club again, then executed a carbon copy in miniature of Earl's swing, striking the ball squarely into the net.

"I was flabbergasted," Earl said. "I almost fell off my chair. It was the most frightening thing I had ever seen."

Earl went running into the house, shouting for Kultida to bear witness to their creation, this tiny bundle of bones and baby fat that had come equipped with a built-in golf swing. "We have a genius on our hands!" he shouted.

Nearly two decades later, he remained just as baffled. "I've been waiting for him to level out ever since," Earl said, "but he never has. He just keeps getting better and better."

This was how the career was launched, the day that Tiger

Woods became a golfer. He had the unsteady gait of a toddler, but a textbook shoulder turn. Seeing the way the baby swung the club, with the tiny weight shift, the tempo, the balance, the hand-eye coordination, Earl recognized an innate gift.

"It is special," Earl said. "It's a God-given talent. I used to ask, 'Why me? What did I do to deserve a kid like this?' It was an awesome responsibility. At a young impressionable age, the slightest miscalculation on my part could have turned him against golf for the rest of his life. There's a fine line between corrective counseling, coaching, and being a parent. It's not easy when you have a gifted child."

Clad only in a diaper, Tiger often chased a tennis ball around the house, striking it with a vacuum hose. The hallway that began at the living room and ended at the master bedroom became his fairway. He'd hit the tennis ball, chase it, and hit it again, which in rudimentary form is the game of golf. He had toys that were designed for the limited attention abilities of ordinary kids—a Raggedy Andy and a Spiderman—but he generally ignored them, preferring his crude golfing implements. Even at that age, Tiger's attention span was two hours, a length of time remarkable even for adults.

Once Tiger reached the advanced age of eighteen months, Earl took him to the driving range for the first time—the Navy Courses in nearby Los Alamitos, California, where Earl, as a retired Army officer, had playing privileges. Little Tiger took along his cut-down iron and emptied his first bucket of balls, then returned home for a nineteenth-hole bottle and a nap—another important component of golf in its rudimentary form. At the same age, Earl allowed him to play a hole on the Destroyer Course at Navy, a 410-yard par-4. He made an eleven. He took eight shots to reach the green and three putts.

Once the baby's obsession with the game was established, Earl began to formulate a strategy that might provide him the best opportunity to fulfill his potential as a golfer. Many years later it occurred to Earl that this was the first time an African American had been exposed to the game at an age that permitted the development of instinctive skills, in the manner of kids who grow up playing basketball or baseball.

Jack Nicklaus was once asked why professional golf had so few blacks. Nicklaus has never been inclined to let a question pass without offering an answer, a habit that over time earned him the nickname Carnac. He declined to let this question pass as well, to his later chagrin.

"Blacks have different muscles that react in different ways," Nicklaus said, causing a widespread protest for his insensitivity. Later, however, he was given an opportunity by *Sports Illustrated* to expound on his answer: "I said kids today are gravitating to sports that best fit their bodies and the environments where they're growing up. The young black kid is in an environment where he is exercising. His muscles develop and they develop to a degree of that type of sport. I think the opportunity is there for young black kids to play golf, just like the opportunity is there for young white kids to play basketball."

Earl Woods had reached a similar conclusion on his own. He had altered the environment to which Nicklaus alluded by introducing his son, at an early age, to golf rather than basketball or baseball. "Tiger is the first black intuitive golfer ever raised in the United States," Earl said. From the moment they could walk, he said, blacks generally played other sports, notably basketball and baseball, until those games became second nature to them. Earl spoke from experience in that he was forty-two when he first found golf. "I was a black kid and golf was played at the country club," he said. "End of story." Blacks always came late to golf, he knew, when the opportunity to develop skills that would enable them to excel had largely passed.

Just as his son knew how to swing a golf club before he could walk, Earl predicted that the next generation of great golfers would be those similarly introduced to the game—soon after they had taken their first steps.

With his parents realizing just how precious their son was, Tiger's celebrity took root at the age of two. Kultida, combining her role as a mother with that of a publicist, phoned Jim Hill, a former pro football player who had become a sports anchor on a network affiliate in Los Angeles, and informed him of the prodigy living in their midst. She invited Hill to the Navy Courses to see for himself, and Hill showed up with a camera crew to film Tiger playing a hole.

"This young man is going to be to golf what Jimmy Connors and Chris Evert are to tennis," Hill said, concluding his report on the evening news.

The bit was seen by a producer for the *Mike Douglas Show*, who invited Tiger to be a guest. Bob Hope, an incurable golfer, was appearing on the same show and he challenged Tiger to a putting contest. When Tiger missed three straight putts, he got angry, grabbed the ball, and threw it into the cup. He then complained to Douglas that the green was not level, that it contained a huge break. An astonished Douglas laughed hysterically that a boy of two, incapable of reading a sentence, could already read a green.

At the age of two, Tiger entered a competition for boys ages ten and under at the Navy Courses, and he won. At three, he broke 50 for the first time, shooting a 48 from the red tees on the Destroyer Course at Navy. He had an advantage however. He was permitted to tee his ball on every shot, a concession to his underdeveloped strength that at that time was incapable of getting the ball airborne from a grounded lie.

In another television interview, a three-year-old Woods was asked how he had become such a good golfer.

"Practice," the boy said, though the word came out "Pwactice."

"How much do you practice?" the interviewer asked him.

"About a whole bunch," Tiger said.

At four, Tiger once came off the golf course with a pocketful of quarters.

"Where'd you get those quarters?" Earl asked him.

"I won them putting," Tiger said. He had been gambling with a group of older boys on the putting green before a junior golf tournament.

"Look," Earl said, "I don't want you putting for quarters anymore."

Several months later Tiger came off the course with a pocketful of dollar bills.

"Tiger, where'd you get that money?" Earl asked him.

"We played a skins game," the child said, confident that he had not disobeyed his father, who had instructed him only to discontinue putting for quarters, but who had said nothing of skins games and foldable money.

"Son, look," Earl said, "I don't want you to be playing for anything from this day on." A few years later, a wiser Earl amended that: "Unless you're my partner."

Tiger's age and race were obstacles in gaining access to golf courses, including the Navy Courses; there, until he was ten, he was only allowed to play with adult supervision. But Tiger did see white kids who were not yet ten, nor as skilled as he, playing the course, which years later he realized was "selective enforcement."

Kultida conducted a search for a course that would allow Tiger to play any time, and she discovered Heartwell Golf Park, a par-3 course in Long Beach, California. She introduced herself to an assistant pro, Rudy Duran, and asked whether he would permit her four-year-old to play his course. Duran asked to see the boy hit a few balls first. They headed to the driving range.

"I was blown away," Duran said. "It was unbelievable. He was awesome. He had a perfect address position and took his club back into a perfect position at the top of the swing and smacked the ball time after time. I felt he was like Mozart. He was like a shrunken touring pro. If you could have taken Jack Nicklaus and shrunk him down to that size, that's what you would have had. It was genius."

Tiger had a three-club set then, including a small 7-iron. He used a baseball grip in those days; his hands were too small to use a conventional interlocking or overlapping grip. "He could, at four-and-a-half, make the ball go high, low or medium, with that 7-iron," Duran said. "He could do it on command."

Duran became Woods's first golf teacher. At Heartwell he established a "Tiger par" for each hole, based on Tiger's strength and ability at that time. "If he hit it perfect, perfect, perfect and got it on the green, five was par for him," Duran said, factoring in two putts. He established a scorecard based on "Tiger par" for each of the eighteen holes. The sum of them was 67 on a course that for the rest of the world played to a par of 54. At only five, Woods shot a score of eight-under "Tiger par," a 59. Duran will argue that that's the best round that Woods has ever played, that today "Tiger par" might be 68 on a professional tournament course, which would require that he shoot 60 to equal the eight-under "Tiger par" he shot at Heartwell.

"Tiger par" had the additional benefit of building his confidence at an early age. Over time this confidence has become one of Tiger's more effective tools. He was seldom over par, even as a small child.

When he was only five, it was decided that Tiger had outgrown his three-club set and ought to have a full set of clubs, cut down, of course, to the size he could swing. He received a set of irons, 2 through sand wedge.

"Rudy, how come I don't have a 1-iron?" Tiger asked.

"You don't need a 1-iron," Rudy said. "You don't have enough clubhead speed to hit a 1-iron. That's why you've got a 7-wood."

The next time Rudy was with Tiger and Earl, Tiger pulled Earl's 1-iron, a regulation-size club, from the bag. He then began hitting credible 1-iron shots.

"So I got him a 1-iron," Duran said.

When Tiger was six, Duran took him to play Mesa Verde Country Club in Costa Mesa, California, a difficult track that over the years has hosted numerous PGA Tour, Senior PGA Tour, and LPGA events. At the par-4 ninth hole, which features a dogleg left and a pond near the green, Tiger hit two shots that took him near the edge of the water.

"I look over and he's contemplating whether he can carry the water," Duran said. "I could see the genius going on in his brain. He never asked what club to hit or where to hit it. He decides how much of the lake he can cut off, then hits it over to that side of the lake. Amazing. I rarely remember seeing him hit shots he couldn't execute. Mozart composed finished music in his head. I saw that in Tiger. He was composing shots in his head."

Woods was already scoring in the 90s on regulation golf courses as just a five-year-old, prompting the television show *That's Incredible!* to feature him in a segment. He sat in host Fran Tarkenton's lap and, at the end of the show, hit whiffle-balls into the crowd. Duran remembered that the little boy was able to do this with the television lights glaring at him and hundreds of people watching, and that he did it unflinchingly. "The usual five-year-old would run behind his parents," Duran said. "He was so poised."

With all the attention Tiger was getting at so young an age, Earl attempted to make sure Tiger kept it in perspective. He tried to show him that his uniqueness lay only in his sport, and that in the greater world he was one of many. Appearing with Tiger on *That's Incredible!* was a girl of ten whose specialty was weightlifting. She hoisted the show's three hosts.

"Can you do that?" Earl asked Tiger.

"No."

"That's right. She's special in weightlifting and you're special in golf. There are a lot of special people in the world and you're just one of them."

He *was* special, but he had not yet learned that he was different. That lesson came on his first day of kindergarten in September 1981. Arriving at his school that had few minorities, he was tied to a tree by a group of older boys, all of them white, all of them taunting him with racial slurs and pelting him with rocks.

The boys were later identified and punished, but the fact that this happened so close to home was a shocking introduction to racism for Tiger. This was the first time he was made aware that his skin was a different color than that of the people around him and that, to some of those people, it mattered. It made them angry, even hostile. He was five and he had been granted membership into the real world.

His first day notwithstanding, he adjusted to school well. Tiger enjoyed interacting with other kids, which helped satisfy a developing desire to blend in, rather than stand out, as he was already doing on the golf course. His kindergarten teacher soon recognized that he was exceedingly bright and suggested to his parents that he skip a grade, to join intellectual peers. Earl and Kultida pondered the teacher's recommendation, then presented the proposition to Tiger, who vetoed this idea. He was already required to play golf against older boys since his game had outgrown his age group. He did not want to be removed from the company of his school friends as well.

School was a priority over golf for Tiger's parents, and the discipline there generally fell to Kultida. On the rare occasions that Tiger earned a spanking, Kultida administered it. Earl often says he never had to discipline Tiger, which is close to the truth. Kultida was the house disciplinarian, and she recognized the indispensable tool she had at her disposal to ensure the boy's good behavior.

"When I need to discipline Tiger, I take his golf clubs away," she said. "He stays in line pretty good that way."

Tiger was required to complete his homework to her satisfaction before he was permitted to lift a golf club. She softened her stance only on the weekend, when, on Friday afternoon, he would begin working on his golf, informing his mother that he could do homework on Sunday. This was her sole concession to the inflexible education-first requirement.

"We're not going to let him become addicted to the game," she said then, failing to recognize the depth of the addiction that already had seized him. "We hope he will adapt himself to school and studies like he has to golf."

For Tiger, golf was principally a summer game, the days long and uninterrupted by school and homework. He played or practiced virtually every day, sometimes from sunup to sundown, provided Mom was in compliance. The notion that he is a product of overbearing stage parents who orchestrated his life is a fallacy; they never told him that he had to practice. On the contrary, they often had to rein him in by telling him that it was time to come home. They were concerned that his obsession might have gotten beyond control.

Kultida recalled a day she dropped him off at Heartwell, Tiger's home course in his earliest years. She told him she'd return at three o'clock to pick him up, after he had finished playing eighteen holes. When she arrived at three, he was not waiting. She asked the starter if he knew where her son was.

"Yes," the starter said. "He went out to play the course again."

His appetite for golf was insatiable, and it fueled his overwhelming desire to improve. Tiger was a quick study who immediately understood the nuances of a golf swing. His teacher, Rudy Duran, often conducted clinics and exhibitions with Tiger's assistance. At one such clinic, Duran tested the knowledge of his six-year-old protégé.

"Where do you play the ball if you want to hit a cut shot, Tiger?" Duran asked.

"Front foot," Tiger responded without forethought.

"Where do you play the ball if you want to hit a low shot?"

"Back foot," Tiger said.

"We did an exhibition at Chalk Mountain (in Atascadero, California)," Duran said. "I'm talking about hundreds of people there, and I'm asking him to hit a variety of shots and he can understand the words I say and the process required and then execute the shots."

He was able to analyze others' swings and cite the flaws. He could identify a reverse pivot, for instance. His own swing already appeared, to the untrained eye, to have been refined and, at age six, he was driving the ball more than 126 yards.

He and Duran played Chalk Mountain after the clinic where, at the twelfth hole—a par-3 of 190 yards—a creek crosses the fairway. A culvert, about twenty feet wide, crosses the creek. Tiger didn't have the strength to carry the creek, but he played the driver nonetheless, and his ball hit the culvert and bounced over the creek.

"Lucky shot, Tiger," Duran said.

"It wasn't lucky," Tiger said. "I was aiming for it."

One day Tiger had the opportunity to play with a club pro, Stewart Reed. Tiger was actually beating him on the front nine, but on the back nine, Reed pulled away from Woods, who left the course in tears.

"Tiger," Kultida said, "you're only six. Stewart is a pro. You can't beat a pro."

She scolded him as well for refusing to shake Reed's hand at the conclusion of the round. "You must be a sportsman, win or lose," she told him.

The same year, 1982, he was invited to conduct an exhibition with Sam Snead at Soboba Springs Country Club, a Southern California desert course, and then play a two-hole tournament with him on the seventeenth and eighteenth holes. Seventeen was a par-3 with water on the right side. Woods unfortunately hit his ball right and it stopped on the edge of the water, virtually unplayable.

"Take it out and hit it again," Snead said.

Woods disregarded the suggestion. Instead, he went down to the edge of the pond and played the ball as it lay, as he had been taught by Duran, who from the outset refused to concede him even a tap-in putt. Tiger knocked it onto the green and took two putts for a 4. He lost to Snead by a stroke. Afterward, Snead offered Woods his autograph, and in a turn that hinted at where the small boy expected his career to lead, Tiger reciprocated by offering Snead *his* autograph.

"I've worked for years to get the hitch out of that swing of mine," Snead said, "and along comes this kid. I think I'll toss my clubs in a lake someplace."

Tiger was a kid, but not in a traditional sense. When he was still only six, he listened to tape recordings with subliminal messages to help him develop a stronger sense of self-control and discipline. Earl had seen them in a store and bought them for his son, carefully explaining why he should listen to them. The boy understood. He played them on a cassette player in his room, hearing only the flow of water down a creek, or soft music, but the messages began to imbue themselves in his subconscious:

I will my own destiny.
I believe in me.
I smile at obstacles.
I am firm in my resolve.
I fulfill my resolutions powerfully.
My strength is great.
I stick to it, easily, naturally.
My will moves mountains.
I focus and give it my all.
My decisions are strong.
I do it all with my heart.

The messages were inscribed on paper as well, and he tacked them to the walls in his room, as reinforcement. He listened to the tapes so often that he wore them out. He began to apply them instantly. He was still only six when he went to the Optimist Junior World ten-and-under division at Presidio Hills in San Diego, his first international tournament. At the first tee, his father reassured him that whether he won or lost was not the point—either way he should have fun. Tiger then ripped his shot down the middle.

Later, Earl asked Tiger what he was thinking about as he stood over the ball on the first tee. "Where I wanted the ball to go, Daddy," he said, shocking his unsuspecting father, who wasn't sure the subliminal messages would take hold so quickly. The negative thoughts that typically invade the minds of young, uncertain athletes were not there. Tiger was nervous—even today he acknowledges an uneasy stomach at the first tee—but he suppressed his nervousness by visualizing the shot, an instrumental part of a professional golfer's preshot routine.

He did not win, but he finished eighth in a field of 150, and the seven players who defeated him were all ten years old. Two years later, at eight, he won the Junior World ten-and-under division. He won it the following year at nine, then won the eleven-and-twelve division at twelve. He dominated junior golf in Southern California. In 1987, he was undefeated, winning thirty junior tournaments.

As rapid as his ascent was, though, he was never in too great a hurry to arrive at the next level. At twelve he was the overall leader of the Yorba Linda (California) Junior Invitational heading into the final round which, for the fourteen-fifteen and sixteen-seventeen divisions, would be played from the blue tees rather than the white. Yorba Linda's head pro and tournament director, Tom Sargent, asked Tiger if he'd like to move back to the blue tees to compete for the overall championship.

"No," Tiger said. "There'll be plenty of time for that later."

He was content to remain at the white tees and only compete for the trophy in his own age bracket. The scenario was replayed the following year and Woods again declined to compete for the overall title.

"That was an example of his maturity," Sargent said. "It was almost, to an extent, wisdom—twelve-year-old wisdom—if there is such a thing."

Sargent, a fixture in the hierarchy of the Southern California Chapter of the PGA and generally regarded as one of the finest teachers in California, had first taken measure of Tiger's talent when the boy was only ten years old. He notified both Wally Goodwin, the golf coach at Stanford University, and Dwain Knight, the coach at the University of Nevada, Las Vegas. "You'd better put this kid in your computer banks," Sargent told them.

Earl and Kultida were determined to provide their son with whatever he needed to maximize his performance and prepare for what appeared to be a great future in golf. Kultida would chaperone Tiger until he was ready to begin playing regional and national events. At that point, Earl would retire from his job at McDonnell Douglas and accompany him on road trips.

The budget was tight and inexpensive motels were the norm. When the father and son traveled, they would often fly to the site on the day the tournament actually began or, at best, the night before. Tiger was then required to compete on a course he had never played. Prior to one such trip, Tiger asked Earl whether it was possible that they could arrive a day early so that he'd have the opportunity to play a practice round, as the other boys had. Earl was angry with himself for failing to recognize the obvious—that without the benefit of a practice round, Tiger was at a disadvantage to those who had arrived early. After the trip, he pledged to his son that from then on he would have the same advantages as the country club kids. He would stay in the same hotels as the others and arrive on the same days, "even if we go broke," Earl told him. Ultimately, the second mortgage and the home equity loan became budgetary staples in the Woods household.

Kultida became a fixture at Southern California Junior Golf Association events. In a mom's effort not to embarrass her son, she watched from a safe distance—a scorecard in one hand, a pencil in the other. She recorded the scores of the whole group and cheered the successful shots of the other boys as heartily as she cheered her own son, a practice that continues to this day.

She never gave much thought to the racial difference between her son and the other boys until one particular tournament at a southern California country club. Tiger had missed a short putt and tossed his putter gently in the air. His attempt to catch it failed and the putter hit the ground. In junior golf circles, throwing clubs and cursing are forbidden and carry the penalty of disqualification. Two of the boys playing with Woods that day reported the incident to tournament officials at the turn, and Woods was disqualified.

Kultida had a passing acquaintance with the parents of the two boys and suspected that they had passed on their own racist

views to their offspring. She was certain that Tiger's race pro-
voked the boys to report him, but nonetheless, she refused to
let Tiger protest the disqualification. She chose instead to lecture him on the trip home. Her message was one that would
stay with Tiger:

> When you've been wronged, when you've been an-
> gered, you need not say anything. Retaliate with your
> golf clubs, your most vocal weapon. Over the years, his
> clubs would speak volumes. *Let your clubs speak for you.*

Despite his relative silence on the subject as an adult, Tiger's
experience with racial bigotry had a great impact on him psy-
chologically and socially throughout his childhood. He had had
his nightmares, as kids typically do, except that the terror that
haunted his sleep was more enduring and not likely to go away
when he awoke. When he was eight, he began dreaming that
he was playing golf in the South and that he was the target of
an assassin. The nightmares recurred for about two years, but
as he continued to develop as a golfer, his self-esteem grew,
enabling him to handle the bigotry directed toward him. "It's
their racism, not mine," Tiger says. It is their problem, not his.

"I've been able to convince him there isn't anything he can
do about it," Earl said. "It's been an abiding principle I've
taught him, that you don't worry about things over which you
have no control."

When Tiger was nine, Kultida decided that he was ready to
be introduced to his maternal heritage and took him to Thailand for the first time. As part of a Thai Buddhist ritual she had
kept a chart on him since his birth. And on this trip she took
the chart to a Buddhist monk in Bangkok and asked him to
analyze it for her.

"The monk ask me when I was pregnant did I pray for kids,"

Kultida said. "He ask me did I ask God to give this boy Tiger to be born? I ask why. He say because this kid is special, like God send an angel to be born. He said this Tiger is special kid. The monk don't know about golf. Monks don't watch TV. The monk said it's like God send angel. He said Tiger going to be leader. If he go in the Army he be a four-star general."

Greg Norman won the British Open for the first time in 1986, basically establishing himself atop the golf world and also attracting the attention of a wide-eyed ten-year-old boy with either a vivid imagination or a vision of a very real future. Norman and Andy Bean were Woods's earliest idols, though Norman eventually displaced Bean entirely and became Tiger's dream opponent. Unlike most kids who see themselves as Michael Jordan or Cal Ripken Jr. in their fantasy games, Woods never pretended he was anyone else. His fantasies involved famous opponents and the fact that he was beating them.

"I pretend I hit the ball and then Greg Norman goes after me," Woods said. "Or sometimes I pretend I'm playing against Jack Nicklaus or Tom Watson."

Ordinary kids dream of conquering the sports world, but Tiger Woods was actually *planning* on conquering it. He was ten when he told his mother and father that when he got to college he intended to study accounting.

"Why accounting?" Earl asked.

"So I can manage the people who manage my money."

That same year, *Golf Digest* published a list of Nicklaus's accomplishments and the age at which he had achieved them. This became Tiger's blueprint for his golf future. He clipped the list from the magazine and kept it in a prominent place in his room. "That was his guide and his goals were set by that," Earl said. The list showed that Nicklaus was nine when he first broke 50 for nine holes. Woods trumped him by breaking 50 when he was three. It said that Nicklaus was twelve when he first broke 80. Woods was eight. Nicklaus broke 70 at thirteen. Woods was twelve. Tiger even had the layout for other achievements he would attempt to beat down the road: Nicklaus was seventeen when he won the Ohio state high school championship, nineteen when he first won the U.S. Amateur, and twenty-two when he won his first major championship. Always patient and focused on his long-term goals, Tiger perceived his victories over lesser opponents in minor tournaments as small necessary steps on a long journey that, by design, would end only when he conquered Nicklaus.

Even as he was focused on his game, he was beginning to look like celebrity material. Tiger had worn thick glasses from an early age but kept breaking the frames, as young boys are wont to do. Kultida decided it was time he got contact lenses. He stubbornly refused, insisting that he did not want to insert anything into his eyes. Kultida persisted and eventually took him to an optometrist. She asked only that he try the contacts for an hour, but when the lenses were inserted, he told his mother that he would not open his eyes. That pledge lasted a matter of moments, and when he discovered he could see without glasses he never again wore them publicly. He had braces then, as well, but they came off soon after, and the toothy, expressive, engaging smile that would eventually become part of his appeal began to emerge.

"A million-dollar smile that cost me four thousand dollars," Earl said.

By his thirteenth birthday Tiger, the golf prodigy, had already appeared on the *Today Show*, *Good Morning America*, ESPN, and each of the networks' evening news shows. As his son's celebrity grew, Earl began hoping that it might provide a means for him to reunite with Phong, his South Vietnamese counterpart. He hoped Phong might eventually see the name, Tiger Woods, and recognize it as belonging to Woody's boy. He enlisted the aid of an Arizona-based organization, Counterparts, which attempts to assist American officers in locating their South Vietnamese Army counterparts.

"If he were captured, since he was such a staunch anti-Communist, undoubtedly he would have been given the maximum sentence," Earl said. "He'd be in one of the reindoctrination camps. If he comes out and he's not a vegetable, there's a chance something might happen. All he wanted to do is to be a school teacher. I'm still hoping that one of these days there's that darn Tiger in front of me."

As each passing year further erodes his hope of reunion, the tribute he paid to Phong by naming his son in his honor becomes more enduring. Tiger was already a name that was captivating the sport and seemed destined over time to become the first name in golf.

The boy to whom it belonged, meanwhile, knew only that he much preferred Tiger to Eldrick.

chapter two

He was as thin as a steel shaft and lighter than graphite. He stood five-feet-five and weighed one hundred seven pounds, which, if a fair fight was the objective, would have required he be matched against a 4-iron. In this instance, his opponent was a heavyweight, John Daly, the Arkansas Player of the Year in 1986 and 1987, and already a legend, on a local scale, for his prodigious length.

The site was Texarkana County Club in Texarkana, Arkansas, on a golf course that, according to a local newspaper, had never before been played by a black. Until then Woods had considered himself only a golfer. Suddenly, he had become a black golfer, which puzzled him. He was thirteen and only vaguely aware of the social impact a talented black player might have on the game.

Tiger was there to play in the Big I, short for the Insurance Youth Golf Classic, a prestigious event on the American Junior Golf Association tour. The Big I created excitement among the juniors: in the final round they were paired with professional golfers. Daly was among the twenty pros recruited to participate with the sixty juniors, and he was paired with Woods. Through four holes, Woods was ahead of Daly, who turned to a friend and said loud enough to be heard by those in the gallery, "I can't let this thirteen-year-old beat me."

Tiger remained ahead at the turn, three-under par to Daly's one-under par. But Daly's four birdies on the back nine and three on the last four holes enabled him to defeat Woods. Still,

Tiger's score was better than those posted by eight of the twenty professionals, and he finished second in the tournament.

Three years later, Tiger was asked what he recalled about playing with Daly that day. "I don't remember too much, except he wasn't a smart player," he said. "He'd take his driver and go over trees. He's got to throttle back."

Daly, conversely, had been indelibly impressed. "That kid is great," he said. "Everybody was applauding him and nobody applauded me. He's better than I'd heard."

Few people knew of Daly then, but Tiger's legend had already begun to blossom and was steadily expanding. He was still only thirteen when his first college recruiting letter arrived in the mail. Dated March 28, 1989, it read in part:

Dear Tiger,

Here at Stanford I'm finding that it is never too early to get word out to you exceptional young men.

It had been sent by Wally Goodwin, the golf coach at Stanford, who a few years before had been tipped off about Woods by Tom Sargent, the professional at Yorba Linda Country Club. Goodwin was reintroduced to the name when he had seen Woods featured in *Sports Illustrated*'s "Faces in the Crowd." He sent off the first of several letters he would mail to Woods in the next five years. Tiger wrote back to him in April:

Dear Coach Goodwin,

Thank you for your recent letter expressing Stanford's interest in me as a future student and golfer. At first it was hard for me to understand why a university like Stanford was interested in a thirteen-year-old seventh grader. But after talking with my father I have come to better understand and appreciate the honor you have given me. I further appreciate Mr. Sargent's interest in my future development by recommending me to you.

I became interested in Stanford's academics while watching the Olympics and Debbie Thomas. My goal is to obtain a quality business education. Your guidelines will be most helpful in preparing me for college life. My GPA this year is 3.86 and I plan to keep it there or higher when I enter high school.

I am working on an exercise program to increase my strength. My April USGA handicap is 1 and I plan to play in SCPGA and maybe some AJGA tournaments this summer. My goal is to win the Junior World in July for the fourth time and to become the first player to win each age bracket. Ultimately I would like to be a PGA professional. Next February I plan to go to Thailand and play in the Thai Open as an amateur.

I've heard a lot about your golf course and I would like to play it with my dad some time in the future.

Hope to hear from you soon.

Sincerely,

Tiger Woods 5-5/100

(his height and weight)

"There's no way this youngster wrote the letter," a disbelieving Goodwin said. "It was absolutely a perfect letter. I called Tida after that. I said, 'It's hard for me to believe that Tiger wrote that letter himself.' She said, 'Coach, he wrote every word himself.'

"I was having a team meeting in my office. There were three academic All-Americans. One guy was being a smart aleck. I said, 'Listen, buster, I got a letter from a little black kid in Los Angeles that writes a letter better than any of you guys in this room can write. It's got capital letters, punctuation, every sentence has a verb in it. It's perfect.' They said, 'Come on, coach.' So I got the letter, made copies and gave one to each guy. Dead silence."

Later that year, Tiger admitted that he was 90 percent certain that he would attend Stanford, although he had not yet even started the eighth grade. He intended to earn a college degree, as a safeguard against failing to earn a living from golf. It was only a contingency plan as he fully expected to excel at the game and to some day win the Masters and the U.S. Open. He already rated his game an A, primarily because he seldom made mental mistakes. On the golf course, he likened himself to a thirty-year-old in a thirteen-year-old body.

His maturity at such a young age led to countless charges that Earl was a stage father living vicariously through his son's success and applying undo pressure on Tiger to measure up to unrealistic standards. But the Woodses simply presented professional golf as an option to Tiger, never a requirement.

"He isn't living anyone else's expectations," said Jay Brunza, a long-time family friend and Woods's sports psychologist. "He plays the game for the joy and passion within himself. If he said, 'I'm tired of golf. I want to collect stamps,' his parents would say, 'Fine, son,' and walk him down to the post office."

Overbearing stage parents were not in short supply on the American Junior Golf Association tour. The AJGA is comprised of the best junior golfers in the country, male and female, and conducts tournaments throughout the year. At one such event, Earl witnessed a father berating his son for playing poorly, leaving Earl shaking his head in disgust. Similar scenes played out at other tournaments, with children frequently walking away from parents in mid-scolding.

"It's not necessary for Tiger to play professionally," Earl said. "If he wants to be a fireman in Umpity-Ump, Tennessee, that's fine as long as he's an upright citizen. There's no pressure. He doesn't have to provide for Dad's welfare. He doesn't have to buy me a home. I already have a home. He doesn't have to buy me a car. I have four cars. I'm set for life. My goal for Tiger is for him to be an upright, contributing citizen."

When Tiger lost to Dennis Hillman in the semifinal of the U.S. Junior Amateur in 1990, his disappointment was apparent. He stared impassively ahead as he and Earl began driving away from the club. Moments later, Tiger reached over and hugged his father and said, "Pop, I love you."

"That made the whole thing worthwhile for me," Earl said. "I'm very proud that Tiger is a better person than he is a golfer."

His mother and father were atypical of the parents of athletic prodigies in that, though Tiger rarely lost a junior tournament, he received the same postround reception from his parents as he did when he won. So Tiger, unafraid of failing and disappointing his parents, had a psychological advantage over those who shied away from pressure and tended to play not to lose.

After a tournament, he and his dad would discuss the round and identify the problem areas that needed work, but his mother stressed that, "he doesn't have to be Jack Nicklaus."

Once when Tiger was ten, he was on the course and was faced with several options on a particular shot. He chose a peculiar one from Earl's perspective. After the round, Earl asked him why he had hit that shot.

"Because that's what I thought you wanted me to do," Tiger said.

"Tiger," Earl said, "you're not out there playing for me. You're out there playing for yourself. On the golf course you're the boss. You do what you want to do."

From then on he understood that he had to perform only to the standards he had established for himself. There was never parental pressure on Tiger to win; anything was an acceptable outcome as long as an appropriate effort was made to avoid losing. Once, his effort failed to measure up, a mistake compounded by the fact that his father was a witness: At the Orange Bowl Junior Classic in Miami, Tiger was leading when he missed a short putt, which ignited a short fuse. He sulked the rest of the round, losing his lead and eventually the tournament. It was apparent that he had quit on himself, the one mistake Earl would not tolerate, and it exposed Earl's military expertise at upbraiding a subordinate.

Earl's lecture, delivered at decibels with which Tiger was unfamiliar, centered on the theme that golf owes no one anything, least of all success, and that quitting is a flagrant foul, intolerable. Even golf's most prolific winner, Jack Nicklaus, was renowned in part for the manner in which he accepted defeat. Even when he was losing, when he was far removed from contention, he continued to grind, as if a U.S. Open victory hung in the balance with each shot. From Earl's lesson, Tiger learned the importance of behaving similarly if he wanted to achieve the same level of greatness.

This attitude was reinforced by the people around him who had been entrusted with his development as a golfer. In 1986, his tutelage had been transferred to the care of John Anselmo, a professional at Meadowlark Golf Club in Huntington Beach, California. Anselmo once aspired to a playing career, but that dream died when he was struck in the left eye with a golf ball, costing him his depth perception and his career. He turned to teaching and, on a recommendation, Earl Woods brought his son to see him.

"I saw so much rhythm and balance, even when he was ten," Anselmo said. "I was awed by it. I knew even at that time he was special. It's like it's destiny. It's so exciting to have been a part of the Tiger team."

Team Tiger was Earl's invention and it comprised a group of people singularly dedicated to the advancement of Tiger's career. The cast shifts occasionally, depending on his teacher or caddie at the time, but the characters remain the same: a teacher, a sports psychologist, a caddie, and his mother and father.

Earl Woods often played golf at the Navy Courses with Jay Brunza, a Navy captain and clinical psychologist, who had also worked with athletes at the Naval Academy to help them focus their attention on specific tasks. A soft-spoken, unassuming man who had worked successfully with a PGA Tour player, Brunza was enlisted to join Team Tiger. Probably the youngest athlete ever to use subliminal tape recordings, Tiger now became perhaps the youngest golfer to have a sports psychologist.

Brunza once hypnotized Tiger so effortlessly, in less than a minute, that Earl was unaware that it had happened.

"Tiger," Brunza said, "hold your arm straight out."

Tiger extended his right arm.

"Now, Earl, try to bend his arm."

Earl, a bulwark of a man, was unable to budge the arm, no matter how much pressure he exerted.

Brunza's first session with Tiger was overwhelmingly successful. Brunza presented a few focus techniques, then invited Tiger to play in his twelve-man choose-up the following day. Tiger was playing in the first foursome, Brunza in the last. Seven holes into the round, Woods was five-under par, and one of his playing partners drove back to confront Brunza, accusing him of creating a monster.

Anselmo proved to be a critical member of Team Tiger as well, contributing about seven years to the boy's growth into a mature golfer. "John was critical to Tiger's development," Earl said. "He recognized and changed Tiger's swing when he had outgrown his swing plane. If he had not done that, Tiger would have been a hooker of the ball now. There was a critical two-week period in there when he recognized the need to change immediately. He was right for Tiger."

Anselmo's first impression echoed Duran's initial observations years earlier; he was convinced that Woods's prowess was genius at work. When Tiger was thirteen, Anselmo offered this appraisal of his client: "He can compete on the PGA Tour right now. He can do anything the game requires."

One way Tiger strengthened his focus was to play golf with his father. Earl wanted to steel Tiger against whatever lengths others might go to unnerve him on the golf course. A decades-long cigarette habit enabled Earl to cough on command, usually a split second after Tiger had started his backswing. A keyring with four car keys and a house key was a useful device as well, almost effortlessly producing a rattling noise. Earl regularly pumped the brake in the golf cart, or jingled his change, or dropped his ball, but only when Tiger was ready to pull the trigger on a drive or to draw the putter back. Earl might warn him against hitting it left and out of bounds, or stand so that his shadow engulfed the hole or crept across Tiger's putting line. He'd make a bogey and mark a par on the scorecard, or use his foot wedge to extricate a ball from the rough.

"This isn't a very nice world sometimes," Earl said. "I've used psychological techniques, things I learned in prisoner interrogation, to toughen Tiger up. It's to prepare him, not to use as an offensive tactic. I'm not trying to create a little monster."

Tiger was infuriated by his father's hijinks, but that was the point. He would have to learn to deal with the distractions that occurred during the course of a round. Eventually he became inured to his father's attempts to rattle him, though in the process he learned how to inject the needle himself. If Earl hits his ball into a water hazard, Tiger is apt to say, "Watch out, Jacques Cousteau." Or on a delicate flop shot, he is likely to say, within earshot of his father, "He always hits these fat." One time, Earl hit a particularly pitiful drive that belied his single-digit handicap. "To think," Tiger said teasingly, "my swing came from that."

Earl often made small bets with him, longest drive on a particular hole, for instance, with the caveat that the drive must come to rest in the fairway. Tiger was already considerably longer than Earl, who was noticeably more accurate. If Tiger's drive rolled forty yards beyond Earl's, but trickled off the edge of the fairway, Earl declared himself the winner, steadfastly enforcing rules designed to toughen his son.

His intent was that Tiger develop what Earl calls "a dark side, a coldness." Kultida was more succinct. "Kill them," she told Tiger. Because golf is a two-edged sword comprised of both physical and mental ability, Earl attempted to do his part to ensure that the latter was also honed to a razor's edge. "I was determined that he'd never run up against someone mentally stronger than he was," Earl said.

From Earl, Tiger learned match-play techniques, subtle tricks of psychological warfare. He typically outdrives an opponent, so he likes to walk ahead, requiring the opponent to watch Tiger, who hole after hole bypasses the shorter drive and continues on until he reaches his own ball. This is a subtle reminder designed to reinforce the notion that Tiger is playing a different game than his opponent.

Tiger attempted to portray himself as a typical teenager, a difficult sell for a prodigy. "I'm just a normal kid who happens to play golf pretty well," he told one interviewer. Yet in the summer between his seventh and eighth grade years at Orangeview Junior High School, a girl asked him out. He politely declined. "Too much golf," he said to her. This was a variation on a theme that has remained consistent through the years.

Several years earlier, Earl asked him whether he wanted to play Little League baseball. "No," he said, "it would take too much time away from golf." He was consumed by the game and was not yet old enough to understand that there was room for diversity.

His television and eating habits, at least, were those of a typical teenager. His TV tastes ran the gamut—a short run as it were—from *The Simpsons* to professional wrestling. When, as a child, his bedtime was nine o'clock, Tiger videotaped wrestling that was televised later.

The fanaticism for exerting self-control on the golf course was not apparent in his diet, which he once said consists of "anything edible." The definition of edible was narrow. It included tacos from Taco Bell or Big Macs and fries from McDonald's, though on the infrequent occasion that he was compelled to broaden his horizons, he opted for pizza. Given the choice between a Big Mac or winning a green jacket at Augusta National one day, well, it might depend on how hungry he was at that moment.

At fourteen, Tiger began an exercise program that he culled from the pages of *Golf Digest*'s January 1990 edition, an article entitled, "Winter Exercise for a Spring Payoff." It was the start of an enduring relationship between two important considerations that joined forces and created a curious dichotomy in his life. Eating and exercise. Junk food and jumping jacks.

By then, Tiger was already beginning to vie with Buddha for space in the living room of the family home in Cypress, California. The room that began as a shrine to Tida's Thai heritage had slowly been transformed into a shrine to her son. The trophies and assorted crystal that Woods had won already filled much of the living room, including floor space, and spilled over into boxes in the garage.

Unfortunately for his mother, Tiger had begun to see the living room also as a practice green. Always with a wedge in hand, he was incessantly chipping a golf ball around the house. But he managed never to break anything, except his mother's resolve to shut down this indoor driving range. He had progressed from the vacuum hose and tennis ball and was considerably more skilled at the practice. He could loft a golf ball over the coffee table and stop it before it careened into the crystal. The surgeon's touch he demonstrates around a green was developed in part around the house, where he had no margin for error. Here the penalty was not a stroke; it was facing the wrath of his mother.

As Woods was focusing on balancing teenage life with golf, he received another reminder that he was more than just a golfer, that he was a black golfer. He was thrust into the fallout from a controversy that erupted in June 1990. Hall Thompson, the founder of Shoal Creek Country Club in Birmingham, Alabama, site of the PGA Championship later that year, was asked why his club had no black members.

"Shoal Creek will not be pressured into accepting blacks as members," Thompson said. He noted that the club did not discriminate "in any other area except blacks, because that's just not done in Birmingham, Alabama." He said Shoal Creek had women, Jews, Lebanese, and Italians. "The country club is our home and we can pick and choose who we want," he said.

The words resonated across the golf world. Sponsors, IBM and Toyota among them, threatened to boycott the PGA Championship. Protests were planned by various minority organizations. Thompson had unwittingly revealed golf's darkest secret. The news media pointed out the paucity of blacks on the PGA Tour and the gap between them and the next black on the horizon, fourteen-year-old Tiger Woods. He became labeled the Great Black Hope, a cumbersome handle with which to burden a high school freshman who was only beginning to recognize that he would be required to play for a cause.

"It isn't fair," Earl said, "but it's realistic, and he is cognizant of his role and his image and how he affects others."

When the Shoal Creek flap began, Tiger was only fourteen and was not asked about the matter. The next day, however, almost as a silent rebuke to golf's white establishment, he shot a 66 in a junior tournament.

Let your clubs speak for you.

Tiger's age notwithstanding, he understood the racism prevalent in his game. He even had the capacity to joke about it, in private. A short time later, Woods invoked his maternal heritage en route to a junior tournament at an exclusive country club in a southern state.

"Dad," the young Asian American said, "you can't come with me. No blacks allowed."

Tiger felt that the idea that he was the Great Black Hope was in a sense an insult. He would not be satisfied with becoming the best black golfer in history. He was aiming higher. He wanted to be the best golfer who ever lived.

This was a matter he would have to take up with Jack Nicklaus, who in a consensus opinion was not only holding the title for safekeeping, but for posterity as well. Woods's first encounter with Nicklaus came in April 1991, when Woods was asked to demonstrate his swing for the audience at a clinic Nicklaus was giving at Bel-Air Country Club in West Los Angeles. After a few swings, Nicklaus interrupted the youth.

"Tiger," he said, "when I grow up I want to have a swing as pretty as yours." There was more than flattery involved; there was sincerity as well.

Even though goals are a private matter to Tiger, he occasionally, and usually inadvertently, reveals his ambitions to the media, indicating how far he intends to take his golf career.

When he was fifteen, he said he wanted to become the Michael Jordan of golf, which made him either the Air apparent or, as the latest in a lineage of next Nicklauses, the Air Bear. He continued to consult his Nicklaus list, but from this list a subset of goals evolved, focused on breaking records. Early in 1991, he set out to qualify for the Los Angeles Open, an attempt to become the youngest ever to qualify for a PGA Tour event.

The qualifying round was held on the South Course at Los Serranos Golf Course in Chino Hills, California, a public facility owned by the tennis great, Jack Kramer. Tiger was one of 132 players vying for two spots in the Los Angeles Open scheduled for the following week. He birdied the fifth and sixth holes, then holed a pitch from forty yards for eagle at the seventh hole. "Don't touch me," he said to his father, who was caddying for him. "I'm burning up."

When he reached his ball in the fairway at the par-5 eighteenth hole, Earl informed him that he needed to make birdie to qualify for the Open. It was erroneous information; he in fact needed to make eagle. It was a meaningless oversight inasmuch as Tiger at that age was never inclined to lay up; he was determined to reach the green in two shots, whatever the situation. But his drive had stopped on a bare patch of earth, on a downhill slope, leaving him with an impossibly difficult second shot. He pulled out a wood anyway. He failed to catch the ball flush and it came up short, splashing down in a pond fronting the green and ending his bid. Mac O'Grady and John Burckle each shot eight-under par 66s to secure the two berths. Woods, with a bogey 6 at eighteen, shot 69.

One of his playing partners, Ron Hinds, said, "You try to avoid envy in golf but that kid humbled all of us. I felt myself rooting for him. I was hoping he'd get into the tournament so I could watch this awesome kid play against Kite and Crenshaw and those guys. After seeing Tiger play, you can't help but wonder what might have been."

A few weeks later, Tiger began playing, as a freshman, for the varsity team at Western High in Anaheim, California. Craig Black, a senior at Western, had worked tirelessly on his game in an effort to play number one, every player's goal, on the golf team. The first time he saw Woods play, he was disconsolate.

"I'll never be number one, will I?" he said to the coach, Don Crosby.

"No, Craig, I don't think you will. But don't worry about it. You'll be number one ahead of everybody else. Nobody's going to be number one here but Tiger for the next four years."

"Here I am a junior on the golf team," Mike Kruse said, "and I go, 'Tiger, who's Tiger?' I'd never heard of him before. Then here comes this freshman that just knocks the heck out of the ball and it was shocking."

Tiger went to Recreation Park in Long Beach for a match, his second as a high school player. Crosby went over the holes with his players before the match and asked Tiger if he'd played there before. Two or three times, he said. When they got to the first hole, a short par 4, Woods pulled a driver from his bag.

"Tiger, you think you need driver on this hole?" Crosby asked.

"Well, the last time I played here I hit driver."

"Ok," Crosby said, acquiescing to a golfer whose game was already considerably better than his own.

Woods's drive flew the green, hit the cart path, and bounced over a fence and out of bounds.

"I thought you said driver was OK?" Crosby said.

"Well, last time I played here it was," Woods said.

"When was the last time you played here?"

"About five years ago."

"You were *nine* then, Tiger. You know, you shouldn't have hit driver."

"I know that now."

In thirty-six matches, each of them nine holes, Tiger was an aggregate one-under par as a freshman. "That was unheard of," Crosby said.

By later that year, Woods established himself as the best junior golfer in the country if not the world, having achieved a remarkable record that left his peers lagging far behind. The year before, at fourteen, Woods had won the Optimist Junior World for a fifth time, in the thirteen- and fourteen-year-old division. He also won the Big I Classic, reached the semifinals of the U.S. Junior Amateur, and was a first team Rolex Junior All-American. His performance in 1991 was even better. Tiger became the youngest ever to win the Optimist Junior World fifteen-to-seventeen division. He won the California Interscholastic Federation-Southern Section individual championship, two events on the American Junior Golf Association tour, and an assortment of other junior tournaments.

The crowning achievement was his victory in the U.S. Junior Amateur at the Bay Hill Club in Orlando, Florida. Woods defeated Brad Zwetschke, 1 up, and became the youngest winner in the forty-four-year history of the event. Asked what it meant to him to have become the tournament's youngest winner in history, he replied, "Ask me after the summer. I have no idea." This disinclination to reveal his emotions, other than his occasional bursts of temper on the course, became a typical defense mechanism against permitting strangers to know him too intimately.

Yet the idea of what winning the U.S. Junior Amateur meant had already crystallized in his mind. On the plane trip home, he asked his father if he could examine the medal he had been presented by the United States Golf Association for winning the Junior Amateur. Earl reached into a bag, withdrew it, and handed it to Tiger. Meanwhile, Earl resumed his conversation with the woman seated next to him. A few moments later, he looked over at Tiger; his son had tears streaming down his face.

"That was a precious moment," Earl said. "I've never seen Tiger do that in my entire life. He realized he had made history."

The victory earned him an exemption into the U.S. Amateur Championship, scheduled for the following month at the Honors Course outside Chattanooga, Tennessee. He would not be the youngest to play in the Amateur; Bobby Jones was fourteen when he first appeared in the Amateur, in 1916. Tiger viewed the tournament only as an opportunity to gain experience at a higher level of golf: the Junior Amateur was his major championship for the summer; the Amateur was just a bonus for winning it. He was more excited about playing with his peers in the Canon Cup, an event pitting a team of juniors from the East against a team from the West. The Canon Cup was held in Birmingham, Michigan, and concluded the day before the Amateur was to begin in Tennessee.

"I may have shocked the USGA (United States Golf Association) office when I said that their tournament was not the highlight," Earl Woods said. "Tiger was shooting for the Canon Cup. It was consistent with my overall philosophy of his having fun. When I said to him, 'What do you want to do?', he said, 'I want to play in the Canon Cup.' "

When the Canon Cup ended, Tiger and Earl boarded the first of three planes required to ferry them from Birmingham to Chattanooga. They arrived in the dead of night, and Tiger had only four hours of sleep before arising to head to the nearby town of Ooltewah, to the Honors Course, a difficult Pete Dye layout he had never seen. He shot 78, followed it with a 74, and failed to advance to match play.

It was something less than a disappointment for Tiger, who had an enjoyable stay in Chattanooga. He was held hostage there by nonrefundable airline tickets, so he, his half brother Kevin, and Earl played golf every day—this in keeping with the guiding principle Earl and Kultida had given Tiger in his pursuit of the making of golf history: the objective is to have fun.

But enjoyment was no longer the only objective in Tiger's role as a golfer. In the intervening months, he had been burdened with a cause he had not chosen. He was talented and he was black, and, as a result, he was no longer playing only for himself.

He was playing for an entire race.

chapter three

By the time Tiger was sixteen, he was already the object of a subtle courtship by the International Management Group, the global agency that represented many sports heavyweights. In December 1991, Tiger went to Miami to compete in the Orange Bowl Junior Classic, then stayed a few extra days to golf with some PGA Tour members residing in the Orlando area. Each of them, curiously, was a client of IMG. For Tiger it was an opportunity to measure his game against professionals. From the media's perspective, it was part of IMG's long-range recruitment of Woods in preparation for the time when he eventually would need representation as a pro.

Tiger and Earl stayed in the lodge at the Bay Hill Club in Orlando, a property belonging to Arnold Palmer, a figure snyonymous with IMG. In a round with Mark O'Meara, an IMG client, at the nearby Isleworth Country Club in Orlando, Woods shot 71 and was seven shots in arrears of O'Meara, who shot a 64.

"Gosh, is this the way everybody putts on tour?" Tiger asked him.

"Hey, Tiger," O'Meara said, "I'm not nearly the best putter out there."

Tiger pondered the frightening reality of that statement for a moment, then asked: "How hard is it to win out there on tour?"

"Well, Curtis Strange won back-to-back U.S. Opens and hasn't won since," O'Meara said. "Greg Norman hasn't won in two years."

As Tiger became more of a public figure, speculation increased on whether his game was already of a professional caliber. "A bunch of people were asking me if he's good enough to play the tour now," O'Meara said. "Yes, probably. Is he good enough to win? I'm not sure. There've been a lot of young, talented players I've seen in college who aren't even playing now. It's hard to predict what the future is going to bring you. But he's well advanced of any other player I've seen at that age. He's very impressive, no question about it. He's rather long off the tee. He's got a good golf swing and a good support group with his family. He's got a tremendous short game. He's very mature for a young kid."

The world of golf is littered with players who, as juniors, displayed remarkable potential, then vanished altogether. Of the twenty-six players who won the U.S. Junior Amateur before Tiger, only three—Gary Koch, Jack Renner, and Willie Wood—won PGA Tour events. Eddie Pearce, the U.S. Junior Amateur champion in 1968, was among the most heralded of junior players in history and played only a few uneventful years on the PGA Tour.

Aware of the prohibitive odds against young players, O'Meara, himself a former U.S. Amateur champion, was cautioning against establishing unreasonable expectations for Tiger. Still, neither he nor the other established professionals who played with Woods were able to suppress their feeling that Tiger was talented enough to endure.

In Orlando, Woods played eight holes with Greg Norman, whom he used to regularly defeat in his fantasy games. Norman, who, the year before, had been second only to John Daly on the PGA Tour in driving distance, saw in Woods a young man capable of making him look like a short hitter.

"That little whippersnapper was driving it by me," Norman said. "We just had a quiet game of golf, but he asked the most intelligent golfing questions I've ever heard from any player. Not only is his game solid, but his all-around presence with questions and ambience is fabulous. I'm just impressed by the guy."

Tiger was not yet the power hitter he was to become, but he was long enough. His was a game that more closely resembled those on the PGA Tour than those on the American Junior Golf Association circuit. On the AJGA tour, he was already an intimidating presence, despite playing against boys a few years older. By 1991 he had won five national events, including the U.S. Junior Amateur, and *Golf Digest* ranked him the number one junior in the country.

But professional golfers viewed him only as a curiosity, wanting to watch him play so they could judge his talent for themselves. An opportunity was about to present itself. Late in 1991, a representative of the Nissan Los Angeles Open phoned Earl and extended a sponsor's invitation for Tiger to play in the event in February 1992.

The Los Angeles Open was the professional tournament on which Tiger had been weaned. He grew up watching and attending it, and he was determined to make his professional debut in either the L.A. Open or the U.S. Open. He had the requisite credentials: a handicap of plus-4 (or 6 strokes better than the handicap of 2 required of amateurs to participate in PGA Tour events) and the ability, even at the age of sixteen, to sell tickets. People were eager to watch the kid being billed as the youngest to ever play in a PGA Tour event (although it was later confirmed that Bob Panasik had actually been the youngest, at age fifteen years, eight months, in the 1957 Canadian Open).

He had played with PGA Tour pros before, but not 150 of them. He envisioned himself winning only by holing every putt and hitting every shot perfectly, which was not out of the realm of possibility, according to an old acquaintance.

On Tuesday of tournament week, Tiger came off the eighteenth green at the end of a practice round and John Daly was there to greet him.

"You've grown," Daly said to him.

Daly recalled their round three years before at the Big I in Texarkana. "He was beating the heck out of me," Daly said. "He probably beat most of the pros there. He's probably one of the first players who doesn't have to go to college. He could turn pro immediately. He's going to be great."

In the pro-am on Wednesday, Tiger played with Paul Azinger and the actor Peter Falk, a member of the Riviera Country Club, whom Woods found exceedingly funny, joking with him throughout the day. The gallery was a harbinger of sorts, the largest Woods had ever played in front of. And it was evident that they had not come to see Peter Falk, but that it was actually a teenager who was playing the starring role.

Tiger had already picked up at least one habit of celebrity, his fans could see. He was used to being besieged with autograph requests, and he had learned from veteran pros to carry a Sharpie, because it writes on virtually anything, even glossy photographs. At the golf course, he was never without one.

When asked his plans for the night, with his debut in a PGA Tour event scheduled for the following morning, he replied, "I'll probably go have a cheeseburger, fries and a milkshake, do a little homework, and go to bed."

The talk of the tour that week was Tiger Woods, but apparently Sandy Lyle, the former Masters champion from Scotland and a man known as Sleepy Sandy, missed his wakeup call. "Tiger Woods?" Lyle said in response to a question regarding the wunderkind. "Is that a new golf course?"

Tiger had an early tee time for the first round, and the gallery started small, but it steadily expanded into the largest of the day. It was an enthusiastic gathering, sprinkled liberally—

for the first time—with black faces, demonstrating the impact Tiger was capable of having on a game that was still on the periphery of integration.

On the par-5 first hole at Riviera, the first hole he ever played in a professional event, Tiger made birdie. He shot a one-over par 72 that was as dissatisfying to him as it was viable to those who weighed the circumstances under which it was shot. He expected more from himself, even while playing against professionals, and he was dismayed that his game failed to measure up.

He played worse the following day, when he shot a four-over par 75 and missed the cut by six shots. "I learned I'm not that good," he said. "I'm very disappointed I didn't make the cut. But give me some time to grow up and I'll be back. It's still the two best days of my life."

He was excited about his first visit inside the ranks of professional golf—still a world away from his high school golf. Only three days later, on an overplayed and undernourished public course in La Mirada, toting his own bag and carrying an umbrella, he was followed by a pickup truck carrying a group of reporters attracted to the idea that a kid could play in the L.A. Open one day and a high school match a few days later. Tiger shot a two-over par 37 in the rain to help Western High take a 209 to 229 lead over Gahr High.

Over the Easter break, the Western High golf team played in a tournament at Rancho Canada Golf Club in Carmel, California. A long-drive contest was held and another Western High golfer, Mike Kruse, a senior, appeared on the verge of winning with a drive of about 325 yards. The range was 350 yards long, and beyond that was a river.

Tiger was last to hit. He swung hard and caught the ball flush. "My god, that's going into the river," the pro at Rancho Canada said. Darkness was descending on the area, and no one was certain where the ball touched down. Finally a voice came across the walkie talkie.

"That ball just landed in the river, so I think he wins," said the man responsible for measuring the drives at the other end of the range. "Who hit that, anyway?"

It was estimated to have traveled 375 yards, neither downhill nor downwind.

"I'm a senior, the long hitter of the team, strutting my stuff and thinking I've got it won," Kruse said, "and here comes this little young punk."

Western High lost the league championship Woods's sophomore year. On the final hole, Woods needed only a two-putt par for Western to win. He hit his approach shot thirty feet from the hole, and his lag putt went about five feet past the hole.

"Now everybody's getting edgy," Kruse said.

Woods missed his second putt, too.

"Now we're going, 'Heck, we're only going to tie,' " Kruse said.

Woods nonchalantly walked up to his ball to tap it in for a bogey, and lipped out the putt.

"Everybody's jaw just dropped," Kruse said.

He had four-putted the hole, and Western lost the league title to Valencia High by a single stroke. Afterward Woods went to his teammates and said, "Well, what happened? Did we get it?"

"No, we lost by one," someone said.

According to Kruse, "Everybody was really upset and coach sat us down and told us it wasn't Tiger's fault. Everybody knew that. We all had a bad day."

It was among the few bad days Tiger had as a high school golfer, but one that reinforced an important lesson for him: carelessness is costly.

* * *

Because of his growing celebrity, Tiger was offered an honorary membership at Big Canyon Country Club, an exclusive club in Newport Beach, California, that sold memberships at a cost of more than $100,000. Earl Woods was meticulous in his resolve to play by the rules, however, and before he permitted Tiger to accept the offer, Earl contacted the U.S. Golf Association to see whether such an arrangement was legal under the rules of amateur status. The USGA's committee on amateur status gave its approval, permitting Tiger access to the course and its practice facilities but excluding him from having voting privileges or the other amenities offered paying members.

Tiger accepted the offer, but several weeks later the USGA suggested that Earl check with the NCAA on whether an honorary membership was in violation of its rules.

"Why?" Earl asked. "The NCAA doesn't have anything to do with my son for another two and a half years. As far as I'm concerned, as long as I comply with USGA rules, what more can anybody expect me to do?"

Earl checked with the NCAA, which initially expressed a concern that a rule had been violated. Ultimately the NCAA decreed that the honorary membership was acceptable. It said that it generally complies with the rules of the governing body of a particular sport, in this case the USGA. Still, the episode raised a red flag for Earl and Tiger, who was not yet even under the NCAA's jurisdiction, putting them on notice that the NCAA was an organization around which Tiger had to tread carefully.

Tiger and Earl were not similarly suspicious of the USGA, which once had a rule requiring junior golfers (with a few exceptions) to have their tournament expenses paid by their immediate families. Otherwise it forbade outside financial help. As Tiger's celebrity grew, the USGA reconsidered the rule, ultimately modifying it to permit juniors to accept "a reasonable amount of expenses" to any tournament. Applicable expenses included air fare, hotels, and meals for the player and one parent.

Tony Zirpoli of the USGA denied that the rule had been changed because of Woods, though it came to be known unofficially as the Tiger Woods Rule. "He didn't have anything to do with it," Zirpoli said. "The rule has been reviewed for four or five years. But certainly it will benefit him."

For Earl and Kultida, it was found money at a time when their accounts were hemorrhaging. They were spending nearly $20,000 a year supporting their son's habit. "The thing that makes it expensive is the fact you have to pay for two," Earl said. "Juniors usually can't travel by themselves. But I've prepared for it. I'm on a fixed income and my wife is working. We're doing all right. But every dollar we get is geared towards Tiger's development."

Their costs continued to escalate as Tiger's opportunities to play around the country increased. By winning the Junior Amateur the summer before, Woods was exempted into U.S. Open sectional qualifying, held at Lake Merced Country Club in Daly City, California. The date of the thirty-six hole sectional conflicted with the state high school championship, of which he was the defending champion. "I knew the minute I heard about the conflict where I would be," he said. "The U.S. Open is too big an opportunity to pass up."

Open qualifying pressure is magnified by the lack of a margin for error. Of the seventy-seven players at Lake Merced Country Club, only ten would qualify for the event. The difficulty of Tiger's task was even greater in that he had to simultaneously deal with the everyday life of a teenager. The day after he attempted to qualify for the U.S. Open, he was scheduled to take the test for his driver's license. And in the days leading to the qualifying, he had final exams at Western High—seven in a three-day period. "I'd come home from school, take a nap until five, then study until midnight," Woods said. "I needed hours of practice, but I could only get an hour. It was kind of a stitch-up job. But I hit it solid. I absolutely ripped it. If I'd putted well, I'd have made it easy." Instead, he shot 77–74 and missed qualifying by four strokes.

"This is just part of the maturation process," Earl said, "part of the game plan. The idea is to dip him in the water then jerk him right back out. He's not going to go in the water and have to sink or swim."

His performance in the Open qualifier was not an overriding factor in his life; he was again gearing his summer for the U.S. Junior Amateur. No one had ever won it more than once, much less in consecutive years, but the expectations for Tiger were mounting. Two days before the tournament began, he was featured on the cover of the magazine *USA Weekend*, with the headline, "Golf's Next Star."

Throughout the Junior Amateur, Tiger's game stood in stark contrast to that of his competitors. The other top junior players were generally forced to play only to their strengths, and deviated from them only when there was no alternative. But by now, he was playing an adult game; he shaped his shots according to the situation, hitting them either right to left, or left to right. Tiger also had a short game that rivaled those of PGA Tour professionals, whereas those with whom he was competing were still developing their games and were not nearly as precise. Tiger won the medal by four shots, then buried his first four opponents, one of them by a count of 8 and 6. The final with Mark Wilson presented a challenge, but at the eighteenth hole, with the match square, Wilson made a double bogey, and Woods won with a tap-in bogey. When Earl walked onto the green to congratulate him, they embraced, a ritual that was in its second year and was destined to become commonplace on the final green of USGA events in years to come. Tiger cried unabashedly, as winning proved more difficult than it had the year before. He had been extremely nervous, which increased the tension, and when he won his emotions took over.

His Junior Amateur victory earned him a return trip to the U.S. Amateur, scheduled for Muirfield Village in Dublin, Ohio, Jack Nicklaus's course and the site of the annual Memorial on the PGA Tour. He was certain he had enough skill to win, but he questioned his stamina. He was growing, but he was still frail, and he wondered whether he could survive the most grueling week in amateur golf. Either way, he knew he would gain invaluable experience at the international amateur level.

In an idle moment, Woods's mind wandered ahead several years. "Pop," he said to his father, "do you think you could live on $100,000 a year, all expenses paid?"

"I'll think about it," Earl said.

The tournament began inauspiciously for Woods. He arrived wearing a cap with a Chicago Bulls logo. At the time, USGA rules forbade players in its championships—other than the men's and women's Opens—to wear hats that displayed logos. He was required to cover the logo with pieces of tape.

"Pretty stupid rule, isn't it?" Tiger said.

He played the first eleven holes in one-under par, then lost his momentum, his composure, and his temper on the par-3 twelfth hole. His tee shot was long and took one hop into a bunker behind a green. This left him a second shot to a green sloping steeply away from him with a pond on the other side. He deduced that he would be unable to aim for the pin and stop the ball before it rolled into the pond. Instead, he aimed away from the pin, to a point where he'd have more green with which to work. When he struck the shot, the ball nonetheless rolled down the slope unimpeded, gravity drawing it into the water. Then he had to walk to the drop area on the other side of the pond, where he was left with a 120-yard fourth shot that he hit to within eight feet of the pin. He pulled this putt and it went past the hole about four feet. He missed the putt coming back and tapped in for a seven.

After the misplayed sand shot, Tiger cursed and slammed his club in the sand. He then missed the putt for a 6 and stabbed his putter into the green. He bogeyed the thirteenth hole, birdied the fourteenth, bogeyed the fifteenth, sixteenth, and seventeenth holes, and shot a 78.

"I think I'm going to go break something right now," Tiger said, as he beat a hasty retreat from the golf course, without even stopping to address the media. His anger was slow in subsiding. The following day, he was asked how long it had taken him to recover from his disastrous opening round. "Dinner," he said. "I had ten tacos and that was it."

For the second round, he played the Country Club at Muirfield Village across the street, the easier of the two courses used for the stroke-play portion of the event. He and Earl arrived at a target score of 69, the number Tiger needed to shoot to make the cut and advance to match play. Woods went out and threw what was tantamount to a perfect game at the course, one of the finest rounds he had ever played. He hit sixteen of eighteen greens in regulation and was on the fringes of the two greens he missed, using his putter each time. He hit fourteen of fourteen fairways and made four birdies, an eagle, and thirteen pars, showing remarkable control as he shaped his shots left or right, depending on the most efficient approach route to the fairway or the pin. He made the turn in five-under par, put it in cruise control, and finished with a 66.

"This is by far the most important round he's played under pressure, when he had to shoot a real low number," Earl said. "He had been embarrassed. He said, 'Pop, I've never been in this position before. What do I do?' I said, 'You shot your way into it, now shoot your way out of it.' "

Making it to the second round of match play, he was eliminated there by an unknown collegian, a lumpy, chain-smoking player named Tim Herron who four years later would resurface on the PGA Tour and actually became known as Lumpy. Tiger still lacked the consistency to play at this level, but his bursts of genius on the course showed that this would not be a problem for too much longer.

By his seventeenth birthday, Tiger was already outgrowing junior golf, and he began to upgrade the level of his competition. In January 1993 a letter arrived at the house from Byron Nelson, inviting him to play in his Byron Nelson Classic later that year. Tiger also accepted sponsor's exemptions into the Los Angeles Open and the Honda Classic in Florida. He missed the cut in all of them, but the tournament host at the Byron Nelson was not disappointed by his performance. He phoned his friend, Tom Watson, and breathlessly informed him of his discovery.

"I've seen Ben (Hogan) and Jack and you," Nelson said. "I've seen them all. Tom, this young fellow has no weaknesses."

After participating in the pro events, Tiger's interest in playing junior golf was waning. He went to the Optimist Junior World on the South Course at Torrey Pines in La Jolla, California, and, in a tournament he had won six times previously, was unable to maintain enthusiasm. A bout of mononucleosis had sapped his strength, and he limped home eight shots behind the winner. He saw his lack of excitement as a sign that it was time to move on to better competition.

The only unfinished business he had on the junior level was whether he could win a third straight U.S. Junior Amateur, scheduled for the following week at Waverley Country Club in Portland, Oregon. "The Junior Amateur is the highlight of my summer," he said, "but it's not really that important, winning three in a row. What's important is just to win it, because it's *the* major championship of my summer."

He again reached the final. His opponent was Ryan Armour, who posed a serious threat to Tiger's reign. Armour had him dormie, 2 up with two holes to play. Then Tiger birdied the seventeenth hole to extend the match to the eighteenth hole, a par 5. Woods's second shot landed in a fairway bunker, forty yards from the hole, leaving him one of the most difficult shots in golf. The pin was tucked in the right corner of the green, on a minuscule plateau. Tiger hit it to within eight feet, made birdie to win the hole, then defeated Armour on the first extra hole. "Under any circumstances, a two-dollar Nassau on Saturday afternoon, it would have been a great shot," his caddie Jay Brunza said. "With the pressure of his third Junior Amateur at stake, it was unbelievable."

The following day, Tiger and his father went to Heron Lakes Golf Course in Portland to conduct a clinic for about two hundred kids. Still a kid himself, he was able to connect with his audience, and his affection for children was genuine. His smile elicited hundreds of smiles in return.

By now Earl and Tiger had worked out a routine for their clinics, and it began with an antidrug message that had been added for this clinic. "Tiger has just smoked crack," Earl said to the crowd of kids to begin the clinic. He then instructed Tiger to hit a ball. Tiger took a mighty cut and topped it, the ball rolling only a few yards. He swung at another and hit it fat. He did this a few more times.

"See, you can't mix drugs with golf," Earl said.

On their travels, the pair conducted these clinics frequently, Earl's way of impressing on Tiger the importance of giving back to a game that had been generous to him. The message Earl was instilling in Tiger was that he has a responsibility to those who preceded him and to those who will succeed him. He not only must carry the torch of the past; he must further a cause that seems to have chosen him. Even though he did not speak about it much publicly, Tiger has a genuine interest in introducing the game to those who have viewed it as an elitist sport played principally by white men, and he began to conduct clinics for inner-city youths on his travels around the country.

"I love doing clinics," Woods said. "I love helping them out. I think that's the biggest impact I've made so far. It doesn't matter whether they're white, black, brown, or green. All that matters is I touch kids the way I can through these clinics and that they benefit from them. I have this talent. I might as well use it to benefit somebody."

He conducted one such clinic at the Douglass Golf Course in Indianapolis. The clinic was for Douglass's junior golfers and participants in the Calvin Peete Junior Golf Program.

"I don't want to be a role model," he told the kids who had assembled, "because it's a hard task and I'm human. I make mistakes. I'm not perfect. But I will accept the role and I will do it because it's important."

Tiger was taught that he owes to golf and to children, as well as to his heritage. He learned to care and share, a mantra passed down from his father. Care and share. The words were repeated so often to Tiger that they became a guiding principle for him in his efforts to take the game to places like the inner city, where it has never been. He once conducted a clinic in East Los Angeles attended by rival gang members from the Crips and the Bloods, who declared a truce for the occasion and agreed not to wear gang colors.

At each session Earl would serve as the master of ceremonies, and Tiger would execute a variety of shots on command—the high fade, for instance, or the low draw. They would conclude with Earl standing ten or twelve feet from Tiger, who would take full swings with his L wedge laid wide open, and hit flop shots virtually straight in the air, the ball landing softly and harmlessly behind Earl. Tiger was already a superstar in the making.

Once more by winning the Junior Amateur, Tiger had qualified for the U.S. Amateur, played at Champions Golf Club in Houston, Texas. For the second straight year, he bowed out in the second round of match play, but his trip to Houston was not a lost cause, because he was introduced to Butch Harmon, the head pro at Lochinvar Country Club in Houston. Harmon was working with Greg Norman at the time, and Earl Woods had decided that for Tiger to elevate his game to the highest level he required the expertise of a pro's pro.

The Woodses were impressed with the work Harmon had done with Norman, and Harmon agreed to work with Tiger. He took note of his swing and determined it would be a three-year project before Woods's game was fully developed as he moved into the Amateur circuit.

Tiger would play in one more junior tournament, an American Junior Golf Association event in Castle Rock, Colorado, but Earl knew at that moment he had outgrown junior golf. "He was lethargic and he was playing terrible and he really wasn't concerned about it," Earl said. "He was bored. He had outgrown junior golf and he never played another event."

Tiger had become the most decorated junior in history, with a record that might never be matched. He was a first team Rolex Junior All-American for four straight years, and *Golf Digest*'s junior player of the year for three straight years, in addition to his unprecedented three straight Junior Amateurs.

Even as Tiger was preparing himself for a probable future in professional golf, he returned to Western High for a relatively normal senior year. That fall, he participated in a skit at a football pep rally in the gymnasium. He borrowed a hitting mat from Coach Crosby, and he obtained a Cayman golf ball—the same size as a regulation ball, but lighter. It was designed to produce the same flight characteristics as a regulation ball and to travel only half as far. Woods was the quarterback. The center snapped the Cayman ball to another student who placed it on the mat. Meanwhile the wide receiver ran a twenty-yard crossing pattern and Tiger, with his wedge, hit him with a perfect pass, the receiver never breaking stride and carrying the ball into the end zone for a touchdown.

"That was probably the first time the students ever saw him hit a ball," Crosby said. "They went crazy."

But at Western High, he usually tried not to attract attention to himself. Off the golf course he was determined to blend in with the crowd, to be perceived as a regular guy. In many ways, he was a typical teenager: he enjoyed school, had a girlfriend, and attended parties. Several television shows asked whether they could bring a camera and follow him around campus for a day-in-the-life-of feature. Woods would not permit it.

"*Scholastic Sports America*, remember that show?" his high school coach, Don Crosby, said. "They wanted to be on campus and follow him around. He never wanted that because the kids might look at him differently. As far as anybody else was concerned, he was just like everyone else. They all knew he could play golf pretty well, but they didn't know how well."

His celebrity was still largely limited to golf circles, though the circle had grown and begun to spread outside the United States. Over the summer Don Crosby was vacationing on Vancouver Island in Victoria, British Columbia, and playing the Olympic View Golf Course. When he informed a few kids that he was a golf coach from California, they inquired about his team.

"How good is your number one player?" he was asked.

"Well, my number one player is Tiger Woods."

Only a few nights earlier, an episode of the television show *20/20* featuring Woods had aired in Canada. The upshot was that Crosby was invited to bring his team back for a tournament, and they had to pay only $25 a room in a resort that ordinarily charged $225 a night. They were also given unlimited use of the golf course.

In the fall of his senior year, Tiger began to explore colleges. To simplify his decision, he limited his choices to three, each with a history of success at golf: Stanford, the University of Nevada at Las Vegas, and Arizona State. The first stressed academics more than the other two, and he had been leaning toward Stanford since he was thirteen, when he'd received the recruiting letter from Wally Goodwin. Still, he visited all three campuses before announcing his decision.

At Las Vegas, he was housed in a nice hotel on the Strip, and he dined at fine restaurants with his hosts, the UNLV coach, Dwain Knight, and a few players. At Stanford he ate dorm food and slept in a sleeping bag on the floor of a room at Branner Hall, a ramshackle freshman dormitory. His host was Stanford golfer Conrad Ray, whose roommate was stricken with flu and occupying the lone bedroom, and Ray and Woods were left with sleeping bags and the living room floor.

When he visited Stanford Golf Course, he made an immediate impression. Several members of the golf team were there, including Notah Begay, a junior who was attempting to hit shots with a Medicus, a confounding practice club with a hinged shaft. Only a flawless swing with perfect tempo will prevent the shaft from collapsing; once it does, the possibility of hitting a decent shot is nil.

"Let me hit a few," Tiger said.

He put down four balls and hit four perfect shots, thrilling the Stanford players, who began pondering the implications should this young superstar become a teammate.

On the first day that letters of intent could be signed, Tiger announced that he would attend the most academically rigorous of his three choices—Stanford—a decision that in his mind had actually been made five years before. Further indication of Woods's dedication to school came the following June when it happened that the U.S. Open qualifying and his high school graduation fell on the same date.

A conflict? Not for Tiger. He chose graduation ceremonies. There would be other U.S. Opens.

chapter four

The night of August 26, 1994, Tiger Woods slept the sleep
of a man who was ready—a deep slumber, uninterrupted by the
doubts or fears that plague those who question their ability.
When the alarm sounded in his room early the next morning at
the Sawgrass Marriott, he rolled out of bed rested and rejuve-
nated and ready for another day at the office.

From the time he could stand without falling, until now, eighteen years later, Tiger had prepared for this kind of moment.
He was in Ponte Vedra, Florida, playing for the United States
Amateur Championship, attempting to become not only the
first African-American winner, but also the youngest winner in
its history.

The air was thick with moisture and warming up, and Woods
was looking forward to a thirty-six hole final in a sweat box—his
kind of match, his kind of arena. The longer a match the
greater the likelihood that his inherent ability would wear down
his foe, especially in the heat and humidity of a summer day in
Florida. He attributed his love of the tropical climate to his
Thai heritage.

He also liked the idea of thirty-six holes. In eighteen holes,
he felt an opponent could sprint to a lead. But thirty-six holes
would take more mental energy for the players, and he was feeling pretty good about his game.

His tank of confidence had never fallen beneath full in eighteen years, and now there was runoff. It was the summer of
'94 and there might never be another like it in Amateur golf
history.

* * *

His road to the Amateur actually began in Thailand months before the summer arrived. He had been extended a sponsor's exemption to play in the Johnnie Walker Asian Classic, a European Tour event in Phuket, Thailand, the first time Tiger felt that he would be playing in a country that regarded him as its own. The best players in the world were going, too, lured by hefty appearance fees: Greg Norman and Nick Faldo, Fred Couples and Bernhard Langer.

That week they were headliners without a headline. Thai newspapers trumpeted the arrival of a native son of sorts— Tiger Woods, son of a Thai woman, a national treasure by his eighteenth birthday. Earl, only half kidding, predicted that half of Thailand would be there. When a Bangkok newspaper announced that Woods was coming, every seat on every airline flight to Phuket that week was sold out. Rather than the many name-pros who were going to participate, it was Woods's appearance that was used by tournament organizers in television commercials promoting their event.

Norman won the tournament, but it was simply a sideshow to the main attraction, Tiger Woods. Tiger opened with rounds of 74 and 71 and made the cut for the first time in a professional event. He then closed with a 74 and a 73, and finished in a tie for thirty-fourth.

His work with Butch Harmon had begun to pay dividends, which Tiger attributed to changing the power source of his swing. With the old golf swing, his hands were the power source, but the new swing enabled his body to provide the power. It took him awhile to grow comfortable with the swing, but it was a transition he knew he had to make if he wanted to continue to improve.

During this time, he had also been invited by Arnold Palmer to play in the Nestle Invitational at the Bay Hill Club in Orlando. He missed the cut and was now zero for five in PGA Tour events, though this did not concern him. Each PGA tournament was a learning experience, another opportunity to measure his game and make the alterations necessary to take his game to the next level.

At this point, national amateur tournaments represented the next level. The first event on his '94 summer amateur tour was the prestigious Pacific Northwest Amateur at Royal Oaks Country Club in Vancouver, Washington, just north of Portland, Oregon. His game had rounded into form, and he had played flawlessly all week, eventually reaching the thirty-six hole final against Ted Snavely, a University of Oregon senior and the reigning Oregon State Amateur champion.

En route to the golf course for the final match, he sat in stony silence. A breakthrough victory in his career was within his grasp, and he knew his game was capable of securing it. Finally he turned to his father and said, simply, "Pop, I'm at my peak."

It was one of those rare times when he admitted out loud that he had his A game in tow, and in this instance it proved to be an understatement. He went out and delivered golf's equivalent of a first-round knockout, throwing every punch of the fight and landing most of them. He played twenty-six holes in thirteen-under par and defeated Snavely, 11 and 10. Snavely played admirably; he was one-under par for twenty-six holes. But he was blindsided by this teenager whose determination to take his game to the next level manifested itself in a landslide victory.

"He played awesome," Royal Oaks head pro Steve Bowen said. Bowen was the referee for the match and as such would have stopped it and declared Tiger the winner on a technical knockout if he'd had the power to do so. "It's as good as I've ever seen an eighteen-year-old play. You hear all the hype of young guys coming up and how much talent they have. But the best way I describe him is that there are a lot of kids who can swing it, but he's an eighteen-year-old with a thirty-year-old mind. He was real fun to watch. He doesn't lose his comfort zone. A lot of kids when they get going four- or five-under, they start thinking about it and hit a wall. He just keeps going."

Woods played the morning eighteen holes in nine-under par 63, with nine birdies and nine pars, and opened an eight-hole lead. In the afternoon round, he had two birdies, an eagle, and five pars, and closed out the match on the eighth hole of the round, the twenty-sixth hole of the match.

Afterward, almost embarrassed at having humiliated Snavely, he did not know what to say to console his fallen opponent. He simply apologized to him and told him, "That's as good as I can play."

Woods was medalist as well, opening the tournament with rounds of 68 and 69. He won one eighteen-hole match, 8 and 7, and, in another, defeated David Jacobsen, the brother of PGA Tour pro Peter Jacobsen, 4 and 3. For the 140 holes he played that week, he was 43-under par.

After dominating the junior amateur circuit, this was his first victory in a national amateur tournament, and one that reinforced his sense that he and his game had arrived at the next level. He returned home to play in the Southern California Golf Association Amateur, a tournament that began in 1900 and had been played uninterrupted since. It was held at the Hacienda Country Club, a venerable, traditional golf course east of Los Angeles.

It was in the third round that he turned up the volume, making a par-4 on the first hole and then making seven consecutive 3s. He turned in five-under par 30, played the back nine in three-under par 32 and shot a 62—a course and tournament record that gave him an eight-stroke lead. Following with an even par 70 in the final round, his seventy-two-hole score of 270 was another tournament record. He won by five. He was building a case that at eighteen he was already the best amateur in the country, and his next two tournaments, the Western Amateur and the U.S. Amateur, could solidify his place atop amateur golf.

The Western Amateur was second only to the U.S. Amateur in prestige. It is played in Benton Harbor, Michigan, and is a grueling affair; the field plays seventy-two holes, then cuts to sixteen players who conclude the tournament with a match-play format. Tiger reached the sweet sixteen, then advanced to the quarter-finals, where he played Chris Tidland, of Placentia, California. Tidland, an Oklahoma State junior, was an accomplished player with whom Woods had frequently played in junior golf circles in Southern California.

Through twelve holes, Tiger was 4 up and victory seemed imminent. But when Tidland birdied the final six holes, Tiger was required to birdie two of them to stay even; this sent the match into overtime. Each player had shot the equivalent of a 65. On the second extra hole, Tidland made another birdie, his seventh in eight holes. But Tiger trumped it with an eagle for a victory in what must qualify as one of the more remarkable amateur matches in history.

Tiger went on to win the event, defeating Chris Riley of San Diego, 2 and 1, in the final, for his third straight victory on the national amateur level. He treasured this victory more than most: he had defeated established amateurs rather than juniors, and it had been on a difficult course.

Before he could proceed down to Florida for the U.S. Amateur, there was the small matter of qualifying for the event, a thirty-six hole affair scheduled for the next day at Western Hills Country Club in Chino Hills, California. He was flying home with his father that night out of Chicago, a ninety-minute drive from Benton Harbor. Because they were delayed in heavy traffic, they missed the flight. The next and last flight home that night had been oversold. They put their names on the standby list, and when their names were called they were mistakenly given boarding passes that should have gone to another couple with the same last name. When the airline recognized its error, Tiger and Earl politely surrendered their seats. Now they were certain that Tiger would miss Amateur qualifying the next day.

But the airline personnel, impressed with the gracious manner in which the Woodses responded, moved them to the top of the standby list, and eventually they were given seats. Tiger was exhausted the next morning, but he made his tee time, then shot 66–69 to become the low qualifier.

Everything in the summer of '94 seemed to be turning in his favor.

It was with this kind of momentum that he entered the U.S. Amateur on the Stadium Course at the TPC at Sawgrass, site of the PGA Tour's Players Championship each spring. Woods had won three straight prestigious amateur events and in each one had contributed at least one round or match to tournament lore. This added to his already considerable reputation. It was apparent that he was on the threshold of establishing himself, at eighteen, as the best amateur in the world. He only needed a victory in the U.S. Amateur to stake a claim.

Tiger tended to focus on his game's flaws and to work tirelessly to eliminate them. His best was never good enough. When he measured himself against his vision of perfection, he felt he had not actually played so well that summer. "I'm just getting up and down, and kind of salvaging rounds," he told reporters. "The only time I ever had my A game was the one day at the Pacific Northwest Amateur, in the final. If you watched me play this summer, I didn't have it. My iron game is not pretty. I'm not swinging well. I've only had it a couple times

this summer and it only comes in spurts. I have not been swinging well all year." He felt that it was only his short game and
the fact that he was putting as well as he ever had were rescu-
ing him.

Yet he was not simply hoping to win when he went to Ponte
Vedra, Florida. He was *expecting* to win. His own dissatisfaction
with his game notwithstanding, he still knew that it was polished enough to dominate the tournament.

He effortlessly qualified for match play, and drew a local favorite, Vaughn Moise, in the first round. Moise, forty-six, was a
PGA Tour rules official from Kingwood, Texas. Several of his
coworkers from the PGA Tour offices located on the premises
came out to support him, but though his corner was crowded,
his putter came up empty. "It's a forty-six-year-old putting
stroke," he said, attributing to his putter the 2 and 1 loss to
Woods. Moise missed a number of short putts, including a
twelve-foot birdie attempt to tie the match at the sixteenth
hole. He hit his tee shot at the par-3 seventeenth—featuring
the infamous island green—into the water to end the match.
The victory ran Tiger's match play record in the summer of '94
to fourteen and one, his lone loss occurring in the semifinals of
the California State Amateur at the outset of the summer.

"He's awesome, a man-child," Moise said. "I'm sure I'll see
him later on the tour."

Tiger won his second-round match, 6 and 5, over Michael
Flynn of Rochester, New Hampshire, setting up a third-round
match with Buddy Alexander, the golf coach for the University
of Florida Gators. Ponte Vedra, located just south of Jacksonville, is in the heart of Gator country, about ninety miles from
Gainesville. It is also in the heart of the South.

"Who do you think these people are rooting for," a man in
the gallery was overheard saying, "the nigger or the Gator
coach?"

The Gator coach was clearly the candidate of choice for this crowd. Alexander was an accomplished player, a veteran of golf wars, and a former U.S. Amateur champion and match play warrior. Earl felt that Alexander had mastered the art of gamesmanship and that he was attempting to unnerve his eighteen-year-old opponent with slow play tactics and other subtle tricks. But the training Tiger had received from his father years before, with timely coughs and jingling keys, inured him to such tactics on Alexander's part.

Alexander was 4 up through eight holes and still 3 up through twelve holes. He had a three-foot par putt at thirteen to return to 4 up. Perhaps it was only Tiger and his father who were not convinced that the match was over and that Tiger was hedging. "He's going to make one more run," Earl said.

Alexander's putt lipped out. "If he had made that putt, it was basically over," Woods said. "That gave me an opening."

A poor drive by Alexander at the fourteenth hole resulted in a bogey that reduced his lead to 2 up. At fifteen, Alexander clipped a tree with his tee shot en route to a third straight bogey. Woods, meanwhile, hit his second shot right of the green and long, and had a difficult chip from atop a bed of pine needles. He chipped it fifteen feet past, holed the putt for par, pumped his fist, then charged to the sixteenth tee box, his own attempt at gamesmanship.

"He was starting to waver," Woods said. "I figured if I showed some energy after that putt that that might get him demoralized a little bit, and I think it worked."

Alexander continued to err, bogeying the sixteenth hole, which squared the match. They came to seventeen and the demonic island green again. This time, Woods's 9-iron shot hung in the breeze and began drifting toward the water left of the green, ultimately coming down on the fringe. Alexander, meanwhile, reached the green, but twenty-eight feet from the hole.

His first putt went four feet past the hole and he missed coming back and made another bogey. Woods chipped to within two feet and salvaged par to go 1 up.

At eighteen, Woods's tee shot again hung up in the wind, which began pushing it toward the water hazard left of the fairway. The ball alighted on land and came to rest about a foot from the bulkhead, but in a hole, resulting in an unplayable lie and a penalty stroke. Alexander responded by pulling his tee shot into the water. Each player made double bogey, enabling Woods to win the match, 1 up. Alexander had played the final six holes in seven-over par.

The match had established Tiger's unyielding demeanor on the golf course, capable of eroding an opponent's nerve down the stretch. He had also demonstrated that he was not inclined to disappear quietly, but would instead squeeze his talent dry to prevent defeat.

Before his next round, a quarter-final match with Tim Jackson of Germantown, Tennessee, Tiger spoke with his teacher, Butch Harmon, who was at home in Houston and who gave him a lesson over the telephone. Tiger was concerned that he still lacked consistency with his driver, and Harmon was able to trace the problem to the way he was moving the club away from the ball at address. Tiger immediately took Harmon's advice to the practice tee.

The upshot was a Woods rout, 5 and 4, over Jackson, moving him to the semifinals, where he met Eric Frishette, twenty-two, from Carroll, Ohio. He dispensed of Frishette, 5 and 4, by playing fourteen holes in four-under par.

"He overpowered the golf course today," Frishette said. "I was very impressed with how far he hit his driver. On number nine I never go for it (in two shots). And I haven't seen anybody hit an iron (on his second shot) on number eleven, either. He flew it back there near the hole."

Few PGA Tour pros attempt to reach the par-5 ninth hole in two; it measures 582 yards. But Tiger hit a driver to the middle of the fairway, leaving him 283 yards to the hole. He then faded a 3-wood high over a tall oak tree fronting the green; the ball landed a few feet from the green. When Tiger chipped to five feet, Frishette conceded the birdie putt and Tiger won the hole.

Woods had made it to the final of the U.S. Amateur, earning him an invitation to the Masters. But this again was simply a bonus that Woods would not allow himself to think about at that moment. When he is within reach of a trophy, his focus narrows, and only winning matters.

His opponent in the final was a friend, Trip Kuehne, a senior at Oklahoma State. Tiger and Earl had been guests of the Kuehne family at their home in McKinney, Texas, a few years earlier, when Tiger played a junior tournament in the Dallas area. Tiger and Kuehne's sister, nearly the same age, had become good friends from their junior golf days.

Kuehne birdied seven of the first thirteen holes to open a six-hole lead on Woods. No one had ever come from that far down to win the U.S. Amateur, and the outlook for Woods was bleak, even after he pared the deficit to four holes by the lunch break.

"How's that for a whipping?" Tiger said after lunch, and on his way to the practice tee to warm up for the afternoon round. "He put a number on me."

But he was unconcerned that this opportunity to write history was evaporating, or that, for the first time, all the energy he had put into winning might not be good enough. When someone suggested to him that enough holes remained for him to make a comeback, he simply smiled. He knew that he was vulnerable over eighteen holes, but few players were capable of sustaining a thirty-six hole attack against him.

Moments before he went to the first tee, his father pulled him aside and gave him a resounding motivational speech that was a single sentence long.

"Son," Earl said, "let the legend grow."

The legend's growth was stunted early on in the afternoon round by Kuehne, who still was 5 up with twelve holes to play. But Tiger reduced that to 3 up with a birdie at number seven and Kuehne's bogey at number nine.

At the tenth hole, Kuehne hit his tee shot into a fairway bunker, from which he could only make bogey. Woods hit his tee shot into the trees, but scrambled and made par. Kuehne was now only 2 up. At the par-5 eleventh, Woods reached the green in two shots and took two putts for a birdie and another win. The lead was down to a single hole.

Woods missed fifteen of twenty-eight fairways in the final but was able to extricate himself from trouble time and time again. At fourteen, he drove his ball well right of the fairway, then hit a low fade around trees and under their branches, the ball running onto the green. He made another par. At fifteen, he hooked his drive into the trees and again salvaged par. He missed the fairway at sixteen as well, but ultimately holed a five-foot birdie putt to even the match.

They went to the pivotal seventeenth, the island green again looming on the hole where land, water, and nerve converge. The hole was cut in the back right portion of the green, a pin placement even the best on the PGA Tour avoid aiming at during the Players Championship. With the hole playing 139 yards that day, Tiger chose a pitching wedge, a Cleveland Classics model, manufactured down the street from his home in Cypress, California. His only thought? "Go for it," he said, as though the middle of the green was a wasteland, a target only for players of lesser skill and nerve. A slight breeze blew right to left and Woods hit a soft fade, one countering the other and producing a straight shot, aimed at the pin.

The ball had seemingly enormous hang time, an eternity to those who watched its flight. When it descended, the only man not surprised that it had come up dry was Tiger himself. The ball took one hop and stopped in the back right corner of the green, a scant eighteen inches from the railroad ties separating land from water. "I hit my normal wedge and it was perfect," he said with a nonchalance that belied the difficulty of the shot. He was confident in his ability to execute it.

"He tried to hit it in the water both times," Kuehne said later. "That's a great gamble that paid off. You don't see pros try to hit right at that pin."

Kuehne's father and caddie, Ernie Kuehne, thought he spotted other forces at work here. "That was divine intervention," he said, "and he's had it for three years."

Tiger still faced a difficult fourteen-foot putt with a foot of break, right to left. Only a handful of players in the history of golf seem to have possessed the ability to will the ball into the hole at crucial moments, and he was among them. From the moment he struck the ball it was headed for the middle of the cup and when it dropped, he furiously pumped his fist. From 6 down at one point, he was now 1 up.

The final hole was anticlimactic by comparison. When Kuehne missed a six-foot par putt, he conceded to Woods, who had become the youngest winner in the ninety-four-year history of the U.S. Amateur. He congratulated Kuehne, then turned to embrace his father, their tears again commingling in a USGA ritual that had been extended to a fourth year.

"It's a weird feeling to win like that," Woods said. "It hasn't sunk in yet. The only time I felt like I won was when I hugged my father."

It was the fourth straight amateur tournament he had won, and, while in each he had demonstrated remarkable golf, most of it remained isolated from the greater golf world. But at Sawgrass he had rescued amateur golf from obscurity—with a solitary shot and a pitching wedge to a pin that invited disaster.

He knew that his skill was greater than the forces conspiring against him: the difficulty of the pin placement heightened by the stakes. At eighteen, he was cocky enough to attempt that shot and arrogant enough to expect to succeed at it. He took dead aim and came up a winner, almost as though it had been preordained. Who can argue that it hadn't been?

When he returned home, he was besieged with mail. A few letters stood out. One was dated September 8, 1994, and was written on White House letterhead. It read:

Dear Tiger,

Congratulations on your outstanding achievement as the youngest winner of the 1994 U.S. Amateur Golf Tournament.

You can take great pride in this remarkable accomplishment and in your efforts to give your best performance. In succeeding at this level of competition you have demonstrated your personal dedication to excellence.

I commend you for the sportsmanship, discipline, and perseverance that earned you this great honor. Best wishes for every success at Stanford.

Sincerely,
Bill Clinton

Kultida had the letter framed and it occupies a prominent place in her home. Tiger had long ago ceased being impressed by his brush with celebrity, but a letter from the president was different. He cherished it along with a letter he received from Gary Player. Another letter arrived from Phil Knight, the chairman of Nike, who, apparently, was not at all offended that Woods won the U.S. Amateur wearing Reebok golf shoes. Jesse Jackson phoned. Sinbad wrote to him. Representatives of Leno and Letterman called to invite him to appear on their shows, but he declined. "That's not me," he said.

His home town of Cypress held an evening in his honor at the Cypress Golf Club. He and his parents were driven there in a stretch limousine, and during the ceremony he was presented with the key to the city.

"This thing tonight is unbelievable," Tiger told those assembled adjacent to the putting green outside the clubhouse. "Here I am only eighteen years old and I'm getting the key to the city? I'm very fortunate to have the city of Cypress do something like this for me. I've been very fortunate to have great parents who love me to death. It's great to see everyone here, my family, my friends. It tickles my heart, knowing that you guys really do care." He was truly moved by the outpouring of support from his hometown.

Tiger's victory moved him beyond page one of sports to page one of the newspaper—notably because of the rare combination of his racial heritage and his sport. The *New York Times*, which ordinarily treats sports as an afterthought, played the story on the front page, as did *USA Today*.

At the same time, golf's profile in general was rising worldwide as prize money in professional golf was continuing its steep climb, with $1 million or more routinely offered in tournaments. The golf industry as a whole was expanding exponentially; the number of those playing golf in the United States had reached twenty-five million, and many were spending upwards of $100 a club for technologically advanced equipment. With its exploding popularity, the sport begged for a bright young star to spearhead the growth. Apparently, it had found its man.

At Stanford Tiger carved his legend from the turf of the driving range. He felt most at home on the range, which allowed him free rein to create a variety of shots. And his Stanford teammates provided a captive and appreciative audience. Ask them what they remember most of Tiger's time at Stanford and, though the stories differ, the stage is always the same: the driving range. It became a favorite spectator sport: "I loved just going out and watching him hit balls," Woods's Stanford teammate Eri Crum said.

The players occasionally engaged in target practice using one another as the target—friendly fire, sharp grounders generally—which broke the tedium of a practice session. One day Tiger, his driver in his right hand, was walking toward Jake Poe, about sixty yards away, at the other end of the range.

"He was looking at me and I punched a 4-iron shot at him and got it rolling toward his feet," Poe said. "He's still walking and in mid-stride he grabs his driver with his other hand. He's got it in both hands now and the ball's rolling at a good pace, and in mid-stride, still walking, he takes a full swing and hits the ball at least 290 yards, a slap shot, perfectly straight. Probably the most impressive shot I've ever seen. Everything in full motion—him, the ball, everything. Incredible."

The two-story Suite Dormitory abuts the left side of the range, and the players talked about hitting shots at it—with a slice, so they would not hit the building. But ultimately they trusted their instincts, which told them not to trust their swings, "just in case you hit one straight," Crum said. "But

Tiger would pull out a driver and throw a ball down, with no tee, and he would hit these big slices. He'd start them right at the dormitory and turn 'em back toward the driving range."

"It's D time, fellas," Woods said introducing his own act, "a little D time." Driver time.

"He'd just put on this show," Crum said. "We'd sit back and watch. 'Where do you want it?' he'd ask. The first time we said to hit it at the dorm, we were just kidding around. 'Take it over the Suite Dormitory and back onto the range,' and sure enough he'd do it, and he would do it all the time, any time he wanted. I thought it was awesome. I figured if he has to get any better than this I might as well quit. If what he's got now doesn't match up with the pros on tour, I'd better quit now because I don't think there's any way I could get to this level."

The Stanford players were required to sand and seed their own divots on the practice tee, and they got the sand from a large plastic trash container, about four feet tall. Tiger used the container for a trick shot. He would remove the cover and drop a ball about two feet from the container.

"You couldn't even manufacture a follow-through," Poe said. "We're talking about the tightest lies. Our range has the tightest grass. He'd take his sixty-degree wedge, hit right behind the ball and pop it straight up and right into the bucket. There's probably nothing he couldn't do with that sixty-degree wedge. Every time I'd go down to the range I'd be totally amazed, until I got to a point that I put no limitation on what I might see from him. He'd hit shots I'd never seen before. It got to the point where nothing surprised me about his game."

Tiger also entertained with his adept impersonations of golf swings, notably those with quirky movements. He had Chi Chi Rodriguez down to the saber dance. Trevino, Player, Norman— they were all part of his repertoire.

He was a bona fide celebrity in their midst, but at Stanford that rendered him only a notch above the ordinary. The freshman class included Fred Savage from the hit television show, *The Wonder Years*, and Dominque Dawes, a future Olympic gold medalist in gymnastics, as well as many of the brightest young minds in the country. In this environment, he was unexceptional. He might routinely hit three-hundred-yard drives, but his classmates could perform the mathematical or scientific equivalent. For every major championship Tiger was likely to win in the next twenty years, a classmate was as likely to exceed him with a Nobel Prize.

He loved school. "It's so challenging. I thought one of the guys in my dorm was a big, dumb, stereotypical football player, a six foot six lineman. He scored fifteen hundred on his SATs. You get guys like that talking intelligently to you, it's pretty shocking. Another guy, who scored fifteen-eighty on his SATs, never studies because he has a photographic memory. My roommate never studies. He cracks open a book the night before a test and says, 'Okay, I've got it.' It's great. But it's weird. When I was in high school, I set the curve. Here, I follow it."

While his teammates recognized his gifts and admired them, Tiger was primarily one of the guys, just another player on the team, even as his ability set him apart. His first year, he was required to tote bags like any other freshman, and he was relegated to the rollaway bed on road trips.

"We've got a room for three and a room for two," Stanford coach Wally Goodwin said when the team arrived at its hotel on one road trip.

"Well, Tiger's a freshman, he gets the rollaway," a player said.

"That's all right," Woods said. "The rollaway's better than my bed at home."

"He never minded that rollaway," Goodwin said. "He was a great freshman. He's the best kid I've ever known. He's a better kid than he is a player. I have a world of admiration for that youngster. I will never meet another one like him."

Notah Begay, a Stanford senior, began calling him Urkel, the character on the television show *Family Matters*, making fun of how Tiger looked at night, when the contact lenses came out and the glasses went on. Woods detested the nickname, which only heightened Begay's determination to perpetuate it.

On an early road trip, a few of the players gathered in a hotel room and phoned Woods's room. Casey Martin disguised his voice and impersonated a local newspaperman seeking an interview. Martin went through a series of off-the-wall questions that clearly puzzled the interviewee. Eventually Martin was unable to sustain the ruse and, laughing hysterically, revealed his identity.

"We asked him all these outrageous questions," Begay said. "He didn't know how to answer them, but he was trying to answer them diplomatically. He's still only nineteen away from the course."

Tiger pledged the fraternity Sigma Chi and was a fixture at parties, though his bid to blend in dissolved once he took to the dance floor. "Mark this down," Jake Poe said. "Tiger Woods is maybe the greatest golfer of all time, but he is probably the worst dancer."

Another of his nicknames was Dynamite, earned by his dance movements, which resembled a man detonating TNT. His swing was choreographed, but his dance steps were improvised and lacked any of the same tempo and fluidity. "On the dance floor, it looked like he was blowing up a house, or pumping up a bike," Crum said.

"It was terrible," Poe said laughing. "Words can't do it justice. His rhythm was terrible. He's got body parts going everywhere."

Tiger truly appreciated the anonymity he thought Stanford

Tiger with his first teacher, Rudy Duran.

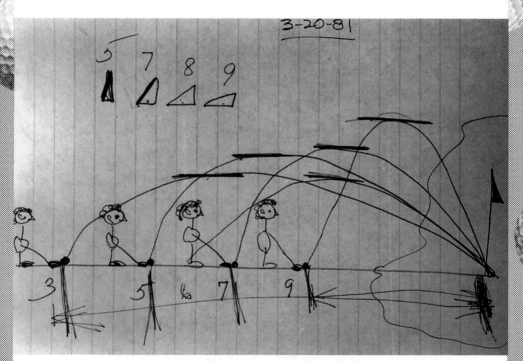

A drawing made by the five-year-old Tiger for Duran, depicting the trajectories of shots made by different irons.

Tiger with his trophy.

The scoreboard of a junior tournament shows Tiger, five, finishing second in the twelve and under division.

Earl Woods with Tiger, five, as he is being filmed for the television show "That's Incredible!"

Tiger. Note the baseball grip—he was not yet strong enough to use a conventional golf grip.

Tiger demonstrates
his swing.

Tiger, at six,
displays perfect
balance during a
clinic. Rudy Duran
looks on.

Kultida Woods
escorts Tiger
to the green.

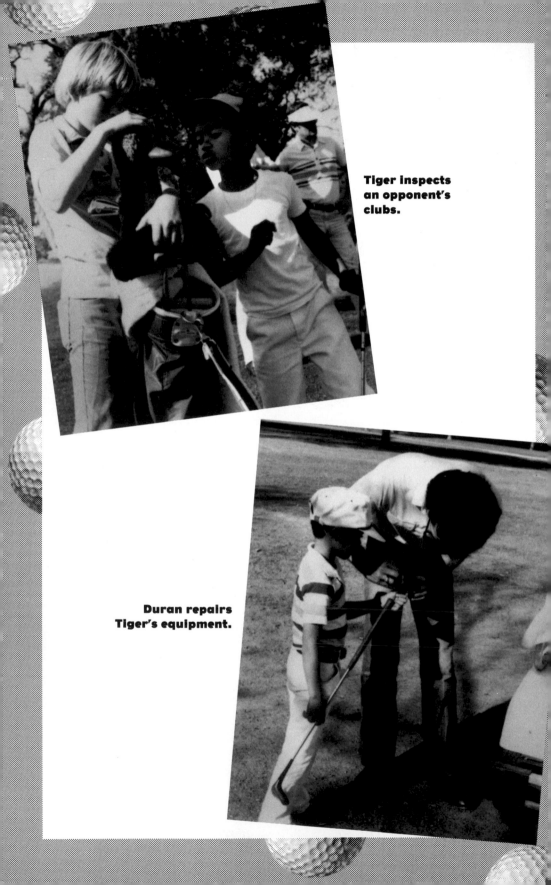

Tiger inspects
an opponent's
clubs.

Duran repairs
Tiger's equipment.

Tiger marks his ball
on the green.

Perfect form.

Tiger at age six, putting with Sam Snead.

Tiger teeing off, with Snead looking on in an exhibition match.

(ALL PHOTOGRAPHS IN THIS INSERT: COURTESY OF RUDY DURAN)

provided him. He could walk across campus without turning a single head. "I'm not a celebrity at Stanford," he said. "Everybody here is special in some way. You have to be special to go here. So everybody's the same. That's why I love the place."

Freshmen at Stanford are required to live among the general student population and roommates are randomly chosen. Woods pulled a roommate who knew nothing of golf and was oblivious that he was sharing a room with a celebrity. One time the roommate answered the phone and heard, on the other end, a man with a curious accent. "Is Tiger there?" the man asked.

"Hey, Tiger, there's this guy with a funny accent on the phone for you," his roommate said.

The accent was Australian, and the man on the phone was Greg Norman—returning Tiger's call—to set up a date for a practice round at Augusta National.

Phone calls from Norman or other celebrities indicated that the campus anonymity Woods cherished was largely illusory. Even as an incoming freshman, he was more identifiable than All-America quarterback John Elway had been in four years at Stanford. Even the legendary Stanford football coach Bill Walsh took a liking to Tiger. "He could walk right past Bill Walsh's secretary and right on into the office and sit down and chat with him," golf coach Wally Goodwin said.

His reputation preceded him to Stanford and was reinforced even before school was in session. The Tucker Invitational on the University of New Mexico Course in Albuquerque, New Mexico, was Woods's first collegiate tournament, and it was played a week before school opened for the fall quarter. Woods closed with a four-under par 68 to win the Tucker Invitational by three strokes, his way of introducing himself to the college ranks. A few weeks later, after school had begun, he tied for fourth in his second college tournament, the rain-shortened Ping/Golfweek Preview at Ohio State, then missed the Cardinal's third tournament.

By virtue of his play over the summer, Woods had been named to the United States team for the World Amateur in Versailles, France. For his son's trip, Earl borrowed a quote from golfing legend Walter Hagen, and urged his son to remember to stop and smell the roses. He also advised him to take advantage of the French culture, but neither roses nor French culture can be found beneath the golden arches, which is where Tiger wanted to eat every meal. He deviated once, and to his dismay, got sick.

"Coach," he said to Goodwin, "if they would just learn. If I could just have McDonald's hamburgers and french fries, I'm okay. But they feed me all those lousy vegetables and I get sick."

"He eats more hamburgers and french fries than any human being I've ever known," Goodwin confirmed later.

At one point in the season, Jake Poe and a few players (Tiger not among them) were en route to a junior varsity tournament in the Stanford golf van. They were traveling at about sixty miles per hour when a car pulled alongside them.

"The oldest, most beat-up car you've ever seen," Poe said. "A long-haired hippie guy rolls down the window yelling, 'Hey, hey!' We rolled down the window. He goes, 'Is Tiger in there? Is Tiger Woods in that van?' 'Oh, yeah, yeah, he's back here. We've got him.' He tears off half a piece of yellow legal pad and at a stop light he hands over this piece of paper. Either me or Conrad Ray signed it, I can't remember. We scribbled out a little autograph for him and gave it back to him. Never seen a guy that happy. He was going crazy. We always laugh about it, thinking it's up on his wall framed somewhere. We probably signed it, 'Much love, Tiger Woods.' "

His teammates frequently sought swing advice from Woods, who spent hours studying the game, as though it were material from an economics course on which he would be tested the following day.

"Tiger lived next to the range, and another guy and I went to his place, and he was watching a tape of the Ryder Cup," Conrad Ray said. "He was studying it. He knew every shot that everyone had hit. He was studying how these different players, like Seve Ballesteros and Corcy Pavin and Tom Lehman, acted or played match play. He'd say, 'Now watch this, this is what Seve will do. He'll try to get into Lehman's head. He'll stand here so Lehman will know that he's standing there.' He pointed out things I wouldn't even realize. He pointed out how Lehman would have a putt, and Seve would go around and stand right there so Lehman would see Seve's feet." It was part of the continuing education of a prospective star.

Tiger's victory in the U.S. Amateur before school began had expanded his visibility, not altogether a welcome by-product of winning. Early in his freshman year, he received an anonymous letter. It said: "You can take the nigger out of the jungle, but you can't take the jungle out of the niggcr."

"Look at this," he said, showing the letter to a teammate. "I'm not going to forget about this."

He taped it to the wall of his dorm room as a graphic reminder of what he still faced. While minorities were succeeding in other sports without such haranguing, Tiger threatened one of the last bastions of white supremacy.

Tiger once had the opportunity to talk with Hank Aaron, who had received his own share of hate mail. When Aaron was chasing Babe Ruth's career home run record, he was besieged with it. He kept the letters to show his grandchildren, a visual demonstration of what he had encountered even as one of America's great sports heroes.

Although Woods displayed the letter in his room, he said nothing more about it.

Let your clubs speak for you.

Tiger has a diversified ancestry, with his father half black, a quarter American Indian and a quarter Chinese, and his mother half Thai, a quarter Chinese and a quarter white. To simplify matters, Tiger generally claims that he is African American and Asian American. To simplify matters further, most of America calls him black, according to its predilection for referring to anyone who is even a small part black as black. This is most offensive to Kultida, whose own heritage is slighted. "I've tried to explain to people," she said. "They don't understand. To say he is one hundred percent black is to deny his heritage. To deny his grandmother and grandfather. To deny *me*."

If a questionnaire or application requires Tiger to declare his race, he checks the box adjacent to Asian. His father has instructed him to claim that he is black when he is in the United States and to claim that he is Asian when he is in the Orient.

On matters of race Tiger has frequently emoted an aura of indifference. "I don't want to be the best black golfer, I want to be the best golfer." He said this so often that it became his mantra. Woods was not given to delivering speeches on the stump. He never recited a discourse on civil rights or racial injustice. It has not been his style to preach, in part because he was a precocious young golfer, not an orator. His forum, he learned, was the golf course.

Let your clubs speak for you.

"Hey, when you're fifteen, sixteen years old, the National Press Club doesn't invite you to speak at lunch," said John Merchant, a former USGA executive board member and founder of the National Minority Golf Foundation. "Nobody has asked him to address the United Nations yet. But in the next ten, fifteen years if they do I wouldn't be surprised. I think he'll become more outspoken. I think he'll grow into that.

"He has a way of dealing with issues that makes them come out positively. It's probably his personality, but it was also taught by his family. He has the ability to remain positive when he's been wronged. That's a trait that most of us don't have."

Tiger was raised in a predominantly white middle-class neighborhood, and his friends were primarily white. Yet by playing a game in which he is part of a microscopic minority, he has been exposed to racism often enough that one can imagine that much of his indifference is feigned.

"Do you feel that, Pop?" Tiger says to his father when they are together on a golf course and he senses a malevolent gaze fixed upon him the way a fighter jet's radar locks onto a target. "It's that extrasensory perception blacks develop," Earl Woods says.

When Tiger played in the Los Angeles Open as a sixteen-year-old in 1992, he was the target of a phone threat, the caller liberally spicing his language with the word *nigger*. In response extra security was provided for Tiger on the golf course.

These kinds of incidents were frequent reminders of who he was—or who society thought he was—and they forced him to deal with it early on. "The young man is about change and I think we'll see more and more of his social consciousness as the maturation process takes place," Earl Woods said. Racism only strengthens his resolve to play better, to use the tool with which he communicates best. It is the eloquence of the man taught to speak with his clubs.

At Stanford he took a course in race and ethnicity, another in African-American literature. He read Dean Koontz novels in his spare time, but there was a time for entertainment and a time for enlightenment, and he came to relish the latter.

"Racism might not be as blatant as it once was when there were separate drinking fountains and you had to sit in the back of the bus," Tiger had told Joan Ryan of the *San Francisco Chron-*

icle. "Now it's subtle, like maybe they won't let you go to the top of the corporate ladder. You see it in different ways today."

In October of his freshman year, the Stanford golf team went to Birmingham, Alabama, to compete in the Jerry Pate Invitational at Shoal Creek. This was the same club that had sparked a controversy four years earlier, when its founder, Hall Thompson, acknowledged that the club had no African Americans because "that's just not done in Birmingham." Not long after Thompson's dissertation on the state of race relations in the city, an African American was given an honorary membership to the club. It was viewed by many as a token gesture on the club's part.

Soul Creek, his teammates called it, teasing Woods. On a more serious note, Notah Begay told Woods that if he went there and won, it would constitute a substantial slap in the face for anyone who regarded minorities as inferior.

Tiger was a little young to understand what was going on at the time of the Shoal Creek controversy. "But from what's been said and written about it I understand much better now," Tiger said upon his return. "I think it was a sad situation. It's not supposed to be like that in the '90s. Isn't this America? Aren't we supposed to be one big melting pot? Then again, it woke everybody up to the fact that this kind of stuff still happens."

The tournament began rather normally; Tiger opened with rounds of 71 and 68, but still trailed leader Ian Steel of Auburn by three strokes entering the final round.

After the first two rounds, however, Wally Goodwin received several messages from a group of African Americans from Birmingham. They decreed it wrong for Tiger to be playing at Shoal Creek, maintaining that he ought to have boycotted the event as a means of protesting the club's past policies regarding black members. The group suggested that Stanford withdraw and leave town, and it warned the coach that it intended an action in the event that Stanford and Woods returned to Shoal Creek for the final round. The tournament director received the same threat.

"I knew Birmingham was pretty far south and something could happen," Goodwin said. "My first concern was the safety of my team. But we weren't about to turn around and fly back to California and not fulfill our obligation. On the very same team is a full-blooded Navajo Indian (Notah Begay) and a Japanese American (William Yanagisawa) and a Chinese American (Jerry Chang), and here they're picking on Tiger. It was ludicrous."

Meanwhile torrential rains blanketed the Birmingham area, and the tournament committee devised a plan by which it could begin the final round without the distraction of a protest. It informed the public that the course was under water and that play would not begin until 10:30 A.M.

"We started at 8:30 and they locked the front gate," Goodwin said, "and that was that."

The protesters arrived, but were denied access to the course, leaving them to protest from outside the gates. The only noise made was by a group of black caddies from Shoal Creek, who cheered Tiger throughout his round. Woods, in maintaining his typical demeanor, said virtually nothing about the incident and tended to business. Among those inside the gates, and a conspicuous part of Woods's gallery, was Hall Thompson himself. His presence was not a factor for Tiger, who shot a five-under par 67 and won the tournament by two strokes. Once again, he had been able to eliminate the distraction and limit his focus to his game.

As Woods came off the course, Thompson was there to greet him. "You're a great player," he said. "I'm proud of you. You're superb." Woods thanked him and moved on.

This was the last tournament he won during his freshman

year. He settled into the routine of school, and although the course work was rigorous and time-consuming, he found the college atmosphere a comfortable fit; he had an active social life that he balanced expertly with his studies. But one night that fall, he was returning to his dormitory after attending a party. He parked his car in the lot outside Stern Hall at 11:10 P.M. and began walking toward the building when a man accosted him and held a knife to his throat.

"Tiger, give me your wallet," the man said, shattering the idealistic yet unrealistic notion that he was anonymous.

He had left the wallet in his car, and the man patted him down to confirm that it was not in his possession. Tiger was wearing a gold rope around his neck (but without the four-hundred-year-old Buddha, a family heirloom, that ordinarily hung from it). The man took the rope and Woods's watch, then hit him in the jaw with the handle of the knife, knocking him to the ground. The mugger then fled.

After the police were summoned, Tiger phoned his father and informed him of the attack, trying to inject levity into the serious situation.

"Dad, remember how I had a slight overbite?" he said. "Well, my teeth are lined up perfect now."

The incident alarmed Earl, who, given his son's ethnicity and the nature of the game in which he was excelling, had always worried about Tiger's safety. "That's why I've always traveled with him," Earl said. At tournaments Earl was a one-man security force who always kept one eye on the gallery.

"Everything that he worked for, it could have been over just like that," Earl said the day after the mugging. "It was a random act of violence. It happens every day. The only thing significant about it is that he knew the victim's name."

The following day, Tiger spoke with Team Tiger member Jay Brunza, who was called on for psychological damage control, to allay any fears Tiger might have acquired as a result of the mugging. It must have been constructive, for that same day Tiger was focused enough to ace a test in Portuguese Cultural Perspectives.

The next time Tiger returned home, Tida took him to the Thai Buddhist temple in Los Angeles to be blessed by the monks, "for good luck," she said.

After getting back into his routine—more schoolwork than golf—Woods played moderately well in the spring. He enjoyed college golf, the camaraderie with his teammates, the fact that for once golf was a team game. He placed well in a series of tournaments—the Taylor Made/Big Island Intercollegiate, the John A. Burns Intercollegiate, the Oregon Duck Invitational, and the Southwestern Intercollegiate—finishing up with second at the Carpet Capital Classic. This was the prelude to the tournament at which he would make his international debut, the most widely anticipated debut in golf history.

He was headed for Augusta, Georgia, and the Masters.

The day broke warm and bright. Augusta, Georgia, was flooded in brilliant sunshine, and the air was thick with anticipation. Either that or pollen, but on that day no one was focusing on allergies. Instead, all were concentrating on the thin young black man staking out a place at the edge of the practice tee. Towering pines framed the tee and cast impressive shadows, but none so imposing as that created by Tiger Woods. Nick Price was there. So were Nick Faldo, John Daly, and Fuzzy Zoeller, all of them consigned to relative obscurity on this Monday of Masters week. All eyes were on Woods.

He was nineteen and so long on ability that he could get home from here with a driver and a 3-wood, and home was three thousand miles away. Home was where the idea of a black man swinging clubs at Augusta National rather than carrying them was not as farfetched as it might have been to a black child growing up in Augusta and standing outside the gates.

Augusta National and the Masters represented the twin beacons of golf's isolationist roots. An African American had not played in the Masters until 1975, and the club did not even have an African-American member until 1990. *GQ* magazine, in its April 1995 edition, predicted that Woods would be one of the fifty most influential people in the next ten years, not for his ability to launch tee shots into the stratosphere, but because he was black and could do so. *GQ* determined that he possessed the wherewithal to drag golf kicking and screaming into the twentieth century just in time for the twenty-first.

More than the symbolic significance, though, Tiger was motivated primarily by the Masters' status as a major championship. As his career would ultimately be measured by his performance in major championships such as this, these were the tournaments toward which he was gearing his game—as Nicklaus had done before him. Moreover, Augusta National features wide fairways and no rough, a lethal combination for a man whose only apparent weakness is a tendency to occasionally steer the ball off line with his driver. Tiger's wonderful short game and his imagination around the greens were important elements to have at Augusta, where approach shots would likely as not catch a slope and run off the green.

When he saw Augusta National for the first time, he felt he had found a perfect fit. His game suited the course: he could drive the ball long, and his tendency to occasionally hit it crooked did not harshly penalize him.

He had been invited to play the course in previous years but had always declined, wanting to wait until he had qualified and earned the opportunity. By winning the U.S. Amateur in August of 1994, he was accorded an invitation to the Masters in 1995, and from the outset he was pining to go. He couldn't suppress his excitement. At home for the Christmas holiday several months before the event, he began studying the family collection of videocassettes on which previous Masters had been recorded. He wanted to get a feel for Augusta National's nuances as best he could from a television set. When he returned to Stanford at the end of the holiday break he took the tapes with him to study over and over.

He also transformed the hardwood floor at Maples Pavilion, Stanford's basketball arena, into a putting green. This was an old ploy; at home he would practice putting on the kitchen linoleum in preparation for a tournament to be played on a golf course with fast greens. His carpeted dorm room would not work as a practice surface for Augusta, which features greens that offer less resistance to a Titleist than an ice rink does to a puck.

As the Amateur champion, according to Masters tradition, Tiger was invited to stay in the Crow's Nest, a suite of rooms above the clubhouse at Augusta National. His father dropped him there on Sunday evening, then as an afterthought asked how he was fixed for cash. Tiger produced a wallet that contained one five-dollar bill. Here he was, dropped into the lap of luxury, a guest of some of the wealthiest and most influential men in the country, and he would not have been able to pay up had he lost three ways on a two-dollar Nassau in a practice round the following day.

His room was just a short walk from the practice tee, the putting green, and the first tee. "All I have to do is walk out the door to use the best practice facility and the best course in the world," he said with a look of amazement on his face. "How can you not play well?"

Throughout his stay, he occasionally got lost in the clubhouse and Crow's Nest maze by aimlessly walking through the building's myriad doors. One such door led into the Past Champions clubhouse, off limits to those without the requisite admission ticket, a green jacket—the symbol of the honorary membership given solely to the winners of the Masters. He tried to linger in the Past Champions clubhouse for awhile, unconcerned that he was trespassing on protocol, his mind probably racing ahead to a day not far off when he might have his own green jacket.

A black in a green jacket is an idea that might take getting used to at Augusta. At least a part of the membership seemed at times uncertain of how to behave in the company of an African American who was not a subordinate. One member encountered golfer Vijay Singh, a Fijian with dark skin, and misidentified him as Woods. In addition, members are enlisted to assist in player interviews, and it was one of Augusta's two

black members who was called upon to assist in a Woods interview, as though the members thought that Woods might be
more comfortable with one of his own.

But Tiger woke early that first Monday morning of the tournament, overcome by the certainty that, despite Augusta's racial history, he had found the perfect event. The Masters is golf
in its purest form. There are no hospitality tents, no intrusive
signage, no swimming pools or tennis courts. Tiger was certain
this would become a home away from home, one that he anticipated revisiting regularly for the next thirty or forty years.

Later that morning, he played a practice round with two
Brits, Nick Faldo and British Amateur champion Lee James.
Tiger impressed them particularly on the fifteenth hole, a five-
hundred-yard par-5. He reached it with a driver and a 9-iron,
then holed a short putt for an eagle—a feat of strength and
talent that reverberated across the premises. Faldo came away
wondering whether he had just been introduced to the heir to
the throne.

"He hits it long," Faldo said. "His shoulders are impressively
quick through the ball. That's where he's getting his power
from. He's just a very talented kid."

At the conclusion of the practice round, they walked past a
horde of reporters waiting beneath the landmark oak tree near
the clubhouse veranda. While Nick Faldo, a two-time Masters
champion, took time to stop and address the media, it was duly
noted in *USA Today* that the nineteen-year-old amateur had not
been similarly accommodating.

This was the first time that week that Woods irked the media,
and they did not hesitate to point out that the teenager had
breached this protocol. But in developing a strategy for han-
dling the media, Tiger and his father had agreed that it was
best that he not address the press until his scheduled news conference on Tuesday. He simply wished to avoid distractions, to

keep his focus on his game, and to contend with the microscope under which he was playing. "That's the rules this week, to make it easier for me," he explained later.

At that particular moment, Tiger had more pressing concerns: lunch. He was en route to the clubhouse dining room where he sat down to a burger and fries and was waited on by a trio of white men. This twist in convention occurred not long after a time when all the players in the Masters were white and all the employees tending their needs were black.

After lunch Tiger went out to play another eighteen holes, this time with Trip Kuehne, whom he had beaten in the final of the U.S. Amateur. They played a spirited match on which nothing more than five dollars was riding. But it might have been a rematch of the U.S. Amateur final given the intense manner in which they were grinding. Woods finally won on the eighteenth hole, doubling the bulk of the estate contained in his wallet.

Originally, Tiger had asked Earl to caddie for him at Augusta. He thought that there could be nothing better than walking in tandem with his father down the fairways during his first Masters. It was not a popular decision in the Woods camp, however. Butch Harmon was among those opposed to employing Earl, who knew nothing more than Tiger about Augusta's nuances. Harmon preferred an experienced caddie familiar with a course that could not be adequately learned in a few years, much less a few days. Harmon was schooled in Augusta's idiosyncrasies—his father had won the Masters in 1948—and he recognized the importance of pairing Tiger with a caddie who could help him read the greens. There was also concern over a sixty-two-year-old with a cigarette habit carrying a bag around Augusta's hilly terrain for four hours a day.

Eventually both Earl and Tiger rethought the idea of employing Earl as they came to understand that it was better for someone else to carry the bag, preferably an Augusta caddie. They settled on Tommy Bennett, better known around the grounds as Burnt Biscuits, who had looped in twenty previous Masters.

Tiger had more than an experienced caddie working in his favor. He was driving the ball long and accurately, and putting reasonably well. "It's just a matter of adjusting to the golf course," he said. "I hear the course changes dramatically from Wednesday to Thursday. It gets harder and faster. So if I hit my ball well and I putt well and get a few lucky breaks, who knows?"

Woods was a curiosity to more than just the throngs who followed his practice rounds. He went through a veritable *Who's Who* catalogue of playing partners in the days leading up to his first round. On Monday it was Faldo. On Tuesday, he played with Raymond Floyd, Greg Norman, and Fred Couples. Wednesday found him playing with Norman and Nick Price in the morning, then Gary Player in the par-3 tournament in the afternoon. They were unanimously effusive in their praise of Woods. When asked what would represent a good tournament for Woods, Norman responded, "Probably to win, for him. He is good enough."

"Certain players, you look at them once and you see something," Player said. "The first time I saw Jack Nicklaus or Arnold Palmer or Ben Hogan or Sam Snead or Lee Trevino I saw something special. As soon as I saw Tiger Woods swing today, I thought, man, this young guy has got it. 'It' is something indescribable. It's the way he puts his hands on the club, the way he stands over the ball. It's agility. It's speed. 'It' is what a great horse has."

Floyd was indelibly impressed with Tiger's length off the tee. "My son Robert played in a college tournament against him last week. I talked to him and said it looked like Tiger had shortened his swing. He said, 'Yeah, he's shortened his swing and he's twenty yards longer.' "

At his much-anticipated news conference on Tuesday, Tiger declined to be a part of the chorus that perennially sings the praises of Augusta and the Masters. He did not speak about the privilege of being there or that it was a moment for which he had waited his entire life.

"When I first arrived here—Magnolia Lane, is that it?—I thought that it was a pretty short drive," Tiger told the media. "From what everyone says, it's majestic and a long drive, you can't believe it, and this, that and the other. But I thought it was a very short drive. The clubhouse is a lot smaller than what it appears on TV, and the golf course is jammed together. The tee boxes are right next to the green. It's pretty much the old style."

He referred to the Masters as "just another tournament. It just happens to be a major. My main focus is on my game, not the atmosphere here."

The press seemed appalled, as even the miscreant rebel John Daly had had the decency to bow to convention when he noted that, "if it was the only golf tournament around, I'd play it every week of the year."

Tiger's comments were lamented as a sacrilege by the media, who failed to grasp that a young black man might hesitate to heap praise on a club and a tournament with a long and storied history of discrimination. Charlie Sifford, the man who had had the heart of his career removed by the PGA's Caucasian-only clause, had never played in the Masters. The club defended itself by noting that he never qualified, conveniently disregarding the fact that the Masters is and had always been an invitational. The slight was not lost on Tiger, who had come to regard Sifford as a surrogate grandfather. He would have diminished the magnitude of the slight against Sifford had he been anything less than honest in his assessment of the tournament and country club.

Sifford was the first to walk through once the PGA Tour opened its doors to African Americans, but he was thirty-seven at the time, his prime earning years behind him. He still won two tournaments, but this only aggravated his bitterness, for the victories confirmed the potential that was crushed beneath the weight of segregation. He continued to harbor this feeling years later, declining to let go of the past, as though, if he did, he might forget it.

"It was tough as hell," he said, his shoulders slumped, perhaps from carrying the burden of injustice around for too many years. "It was a tough proposition." Sifford was taken aback at the suggestion that he and those who followed him—men such as Lee Elder, Calvin Peete, Pete Brown, Jim Thorpe, and Jim Dent—had forged a trail that would remove Woods's burden. "He's still black, isn't he?" Sifford said tersely. "Let me tell you something about golf. There are some white people in this world today that don't believe black men should be playing golf."

Nevertheless, Sifford believed in Tiger's ability to carve a place for himself in golf history. "He might be the best black player since Teddy Rhodes. This is the way it should have been when I played. He's part of the system. I like his chances, I really like his chances."

Earl Woods also knew something about breaking new ground. He had been the first black baseball player in the history of the Big Eight Conference (then the Big Seven), at Kansas State University. When the team played the University of Oklahoma in Norman, Earl was not welcome in the hotel where the rest of the team stayed. He stayed in Oklahoma City in a hotel for "Negroes." Often he was forced to eat his meals in restaurant parking lots, because he was not welcome to join his teammates dining inside.

Tiger had been taught the history of blacks in golf by his

father, who did not advocate walking through life wearing blinders as though racism was now completely removed from the game. He was determined that his progeny be aware of the injustices endured and the sacrifices made by the black golfers who preceded him. Earl told him stories of the legendary Teddy Rhodes, often considered the best black golfer in history, though he played during the time that the Caucasian-only rule was in force on the PGA Tour, and when tournaments called "opens" were not open at all.

"I believe he was the best there ever was, and I don't mean among the black players," Charlie Sifford wrote in his book, *Just Let Me Play*. "From 1945 to 1950, Teddy Rhodes was as good a golfer as anyone on the planet. But nobody ever heard of him, because he was black."

Tiger had heard of him, though, because Earl deemed it so important. "I've taught that young man black history," Earl said, "so that he can know and appreciate those who came before him and made it possible for him to walk down that fairway."

He made sure that his son was taught the history of Augusta National and the Masters, each an icon of Southern segregation for years after the Civil Rights movement had begun. Before he ever arrived in Georgia, Tiger learned that no black man had played in the Masters until 1975 and that Charlie Sifford was denied the opportunity to compete there. He knew that historically a black man was allowed to enter the hallowed grounds of Augusta National only through the employee gate. He was aware that Augusta National had not welcomed a black member until 1990, and only after Hall Thompson's comments on Shoal Creek's membership policy.

Shoal Creek was not unique in this regard, prompting both the PGA Tour and the U.S. Golf Association to pass down an edict that they would no longer permit their events to be held on courses that discriminate. Augusta National complied, although its membership insisted that it was in the process of integrating prior to the Shoal Creek flap.

The subject of race and the club's history is not a popular subject among the membership. A stridently private club that only reluctantly opens its doors to the world for one week a year, Augusta National prefers that club matters remain private, particularly those of a racial bent, for they tend to reinforce the unflattering reputation.

The club has two black members. The second to join was Billy Simms, a Charlotte, North Carolina, businessman who had been a track star at the University of Southern California. A reporter phoned Simms to ask him his opinion on the impact of Woods's participation in the Masters.

"Probably the same as anybody else," he said. Pressed on the matter, he said, "Am I missing something here?"

It was as though the club's bylaws precluded members from acknowledging the past. "The average golfer that goes there is blown away with Magnolia Lane and the history and tradition of the Masters," Earl Woods said. "That doesn't impress the black golfer."

But when Tiger arrived at the Augusta National clubhouse on the morning of the first round, he was not dwelling on the past. Typically he was focused on the round ahead of him to be played on a course he had already grown to love. A telegram was waiting for him in the clubhouse from Sifford, who wished him luck and instructed him to focus on playing his best golf and to ignore the significance that others were attaching to his appearance at Augusta.

Rain pelted Augusta National that morning but did not diminish the enthusiasm of the crowd huddled around the first tee, awaiting the announcement signaling the beginning of a new era in Masters history.

"Fore, please," the starter announced. "Tiger Woods now driving."

Golf's most anticipated moment of the year had arrived and, in a matter of a few seconds, many in the crowd wondered whether they had witnessed the second coming—of Nicklaus. Woods struck his tee shot down the right side, over the distant bunker that forces lesser players to steer clear of the trouble by aiming left.

"I needed binoculars to see where he hit the ball," said defending champion Jose Maria Olazabal, Tiger's playing partner and latest convert. "On the first hole he flew his drive over the bunker on the right side, 280 yards on the fly."

He hit an indifferent second shot that stopped thirty feet right of the hole, setting up his first putt in earnest on greens that made the Maples Pavilion hardwood seem like an uphill slope. His first putt began rolling and showed no inclination toward applying the brakes anytime soon. It went past the pin, caught a downslope, and rolled off the green, fifty feet from the pin—a thirty-foot lag putt that netted a minus-twenty feet. He then chipped onto the green, twelve feet from the hole, and made the putt for bogey.

It was a minor glitch on an uneventful day. Tiger shot an even-par 72 that was four strokes better than Nicklaus and Palmer had shot in their Masters debuts, but it was notable for nothing else. He was tied for thirty-fourth.

"It was a good start to the tournament," Woods said, "I drove the ball very well. I didn't want to lose focus. More than anything, I kept saying, 'the game hasn't changed.' "

On Friday, Tiger shot another 72 and made the cut for the first time in a PGA Tour event. Watching the round was Hall Thompson himself. An Augusta National member, Thompson was wearing the green jacket that indicates membership in the club. Adjacent to the fifth fairway, Earl Woods was perched atop his shooting stick watching his son play the fifth hole when Thompson approached him.

"Were you at Shoal Creek for the college tournament?" Thompson asked Earl, who was not yet aware of the man's identity.

"No, I wasn't," Earl said.

"Your son played beautifully," Thompson said. "By the way, I'm Hall Thompson. I'm the founder of Shoal Creek."

Earl stared impassively ahead, declining to acknowledge the man. Whether Thompson was genuinely remorseful or exercising damage control was a moot point to Earl.

As Earl said later, "Shoal Creek will forever be tarnished."

At six on Friday evening, at the conclusion of his second round, Tiger, still in his golf shoes, departed the hallowed grounds of Augusta National for a short trip to the other side of the tracks, a scruffy municipal course, Forest Hills Golf Club. He met with the Masters' erstwhile caddies, all black, and he conducted a clinic for a group of black children. Until 1982, Masters competitors were required to use an Augusta National caddie, but once they were permitted to bring their own caddies, the men from Augusta were largely forgotten. He wanted to pay his respects to these former caddies, one of who wore a T-shirt that day that said, "Without black history, there is no history."

"This is great," one former caddie, Jerry Beard, said of Tiger's participation in the Masters. "It's a great thing for golf, and it's great especially for black youth. It's good for kids to see you can get into something like this, to see that they can play golf."

Tiger staged a clinic for the kids, then sat down with the caddies, whose enthusiasm was etched on their beaming faces.

Here was a man who had made it inside the ropes—not to carry another golfer's bag, but as a bona fide player.

"This is part of the process," Tiger said to them. "My dad has always taught me these words: care and share. That's why we put on clinics. The only thing I can do is try to give back. If it works, it works."

"I'm so proud of you," one former caddie said. "All of Augusta is. We're all so proud of you."

None of them were as proud as Earl, who said, "This is the culmination of a very hectic, long day, and, I might add, a very proud day in the Woods family. This young man has made his first cut in a PGA tournament, and he made it in a major championship. I've watched this young man pass from adolescence to manhood, and I'm very proud of him."

"Thanks, Pop," Tiger said.

Tiger might have been there primarily through the urging of his father, but he was there, and enjoying it. It was part of his training. Earl was determined that Tiger understand his obligation to the cause.

"It's a black thing," Earl said. "We are acknowledging that we know who came before Tiger, and that they suffered humiliation and that we realize the debt. It's a way of saying thank you and a promise to carry the baton."

After Tiger spoke, Earl delivered a send-off: "We need a Technicolor green jacket," he said to them, "a black in a green jacket. It is time. The day has come and it's long overdue. I promise you it will happen."

Back at Augusta, a five-over par 77 in the third round effectively removed Tiger from contention for that year's event, and he was left to play for pride in the final round on Sunday. Saturday afternoon he went to the practice tee, where he occupied a place next to Davis Love III, who had led the PGA Tour in driving distance the previous year. Love pulled his driver from the bag and was exhorted by the crowd to attempt to carry the fifty-foot-high net at the end of the range, 260 yards away. The net is there to protect Washington Road from a barrage of range balls. Love hit two drives that bounded off the net. Woods looked at Love and asked, "Should I try?" Love nodded. Woods pulled the headcover from his driver, teed up a ball, then unleashed a drive that sailed effortlessly over the netting, a tape measure home run that caused the spectators to applaud enthusiastically.

All week Tiger put on a display of power seldom seen at Augusta National. "Ain't enough golf course out there for him," Burnt Biscuits said. The course was hard and fast, and unlike John Daly, whose drives fly high and land soft, Tiger hit boring drives that, once they touched down, ran like frightened cats. He averaged 311 yards per drive for the week to lead the field.

His driving prowess notwithstanding, Tiger came to understand why Augusta National is called a second-shot course. Woods's length off the tee left him with countless short-iron shots to the greens, an advantage he was unable to utilize. It exposed a flaw in his repertoire: an inability to control the distance on his short irons. Using them the way he does his other clubs, with little in reserve, he kept flying the greens.

"Driving here is not the hard part," Woods said. "It's pretty much the easy part. It's a second-shot golf course, as everyone says. The way the greens are right now, it's very difficult to hold shots. The first hop the ball takes is very big and it's going to take a little time getting adjusted to that."

As Tiger left the course after his round of 77 on Saturday, he was dejected. He encountered Earl by the clubhouse veranda and sought his advice on how to correct this flaw. They engaged in a spirited, and somewhat profane, public debate. At one point Earl suggested that Tiger aim for the front of the greens to compensate. Eventually they decided that Tiger should replace his Mizuno irons, 6 through pitching wedge, with the Cobra irons that belonged to his teacher, Butch Harmon.

One of Harmon's traits is that he does not mince words. He has never shied from dispensing an earful to a client, even Greg Norman. For the truth, you go to Harmon. And Woods sought the truth that afternoon on the practice tee. He wanted to know how his game compared with those of the best players in the world.

"You're almost there now," Harmon said, high praise indeed.

"How long do you think it'll take?" Woods asked.

"With your work ethic, less than a year."

But he wasn't there yet. On Sunday, with Woods hopelessly out of contention, he shot another even-par 72 that included three birdies on the final four holes. He finished in a tie for forty-first, which fell somewhere between disappointment and elation. He had not embarrassed himself, but neither had he played to his potential.

After he was finished playing in the tournament, he wrote a letter to the officers, tournament staff, and membership at Augusta National, and read it to the media:

> Please accept my sincere thanks for providing me the opportunity to experience the most wonderful week of my life. It was Fantasyland and Disney World wrapped into one.
>
> I was treated like a gentleman throughout my stay and I trust I responded in kind. The Crow's Nest will always remain in my heart and your magnificent golf course will provide a continuing challenge throughout my amateur and professional career.
>
> I've accomplished much here and learned even

more. Your tournament will always hold a special spot in my heart as the place where I made my first PGA cut and at a major yet! It is here that I left my youth behind and became a man. For that I will be eternally in your debt.

> With warmest regards and
> deepest appreciation,
> Sincerely,
> Tiger Woods

A few in the media snickered, condemning the letter as propaganda orchestrated by his father. The less cynical felt that Tiger's graciousness was a noble undertaking. Among them was Scott Ostler, a columnist with the *San Francisco Chronicle*, who wrote about the letter and the clinic that Woods had conducted for Augusta's caddies and neighborhood kids:

> The letter and the clinic smack ominously of a father instilling values in his son. Almost 900 golfers have played in 59 Masters tournaments, and only one of them has taken the time to give a clinic at that frumpy muni course.

The week was over and Tiger rated it a success, if less than a smashing one. Harmon wondered what might have been if he had exercised distance control with his short irons. "He might have been in contention," he said. Tiger was the only amateur to make the cut; he was also the only participant required to read a history textbook at night following a long day of work.

Hours after he returned to Palo Alto, he had a history exam.

A few weeks after the tournament, Tiger received a letter from Jackson Stephens, the Masters chairman. He congratulated Woods on being the low amateur and for the manner in which he had conducted himself on and off the course. He said he expected Woods to return for the Masters in 1996 and looked forward to getting to know him better in the future.

Another Augusta member, Charles Yates, the pressroom co-ordinator, wrote a similar note to Woods. They were reaching out to embrace the future, a curious turn for a club that had steadfastly resisted doing so over the years.

As for Tiger, he saw a course that suited his game, and a major championship—an appealing combination. He was already looking forward to going back.

Meanwhile a letter arrived at the Woods's house in Cypress, California. The envelope was innocuous, though the lack of a return address may have hinted at the contents. It was post-marked in Florida, addressed to Tiger Woods, and mailed to him in care of the Augusta National Golf Club, Augusta, Georgia. The letter was one of many sent to Tiger at the club and subsequently forwarded to the Woods residence in California. Tiger's mother often handled the fan mail in his absence, and since he was away at school, she opened this letter as well. It contained a single sentence, typed, and, typical of these kinds of letters, it was anonymous. It read:

"Just what we don't need, another nigger in sports."

chapter seven

In a sense Tiger is hunting neither trophies nor money, though he is certain to accumulate a warehouse full of each. He is hunting big game, the Golden Bear, Jack Nicklaus, a man who represents all that Woods wishes to accomplish in golf. He will measure each of his achievements against those of Nicklaus, who is recognized as the greatest player in history—the same title to which Tiger aspires. To wrest it from him, he will have to systematically trump each installment on Nicklaus's record.

Even at the college level the specter of Nicklaus was in full force: Nicklaus was one of only two players ever to win the NCAA Championship and the U.S. Amateur in the same year (the other was Phil Mickelson). The spring of his freshman year and the summer that followed gave Tiger his first opportunity to duplicate the feat. It began on Nicklaus's home turf, on the Scarlet Course at Ohio State, Nicklaus's college, and in his hometown, Columbus.

Tiger thought that the first half of the NCAA–U.S. Amateur double would be the easier of the two, since only college players were involved; moreover, he had already been ordained the greatest college player in history by Oklahoma State coach Mike Holder. "He's the best of all time," Holder said. "His record backs it up. There's never been a player at this stage of his career who has done what Tiger Woods has done."

The statement might have been just Holder's putting the pressure on Tiger to perform beyond himself. Oklahoma State and defending champion Stanford were expected to vie for the team title, and Holder may have been invoking the we-have-nothing-to-lose strategy.

Tiger's desire to win the NCAA was hampered by the reality that he had not had an adequate opportunity to hone his game. A series of injuries and illnesses had dogged him in recent months, affecting his ability to practice and raising the question of his fragility as an athlete. He was breaking down physically with alarming regularity. Although his father had taught him "to listen to his body," the suspicion among the media was that he listened too closely. He was raised to pay attention to aches and pains; the remedy he learned from his father was to quit playing for awhile. The previous winter he had undergone arthroscopic surgery on his knee. At the Masters he left the course six holes into his final practice round with a spasm in his lower back and went to the PGA Tour fitness van to receive treatment. On his first drive of the second round of the U.S. Intercollegiate at Stanford, with more than seven hundred in attendance—the largest crowd ever to watch a golf tournament at Stanford—he strained his right rotator cuff and played only eleven holes before leaving the course and withdrawing from the tournament. That particular injury had predated the Masters, Earl Woods said, but Tiger had declined to inform anyone about it before. It ultimately prevented him from participating in the Pacific 10 Championship.

At the NCAA West Regional two weeks later, he suffered from a stomach disorder on the first day. Unfortunately for Stanford, teammate Casey Martin was similarly stricken and had already withdrawn. Had Woods withdrawn as well, Stanford would have been disqualified as a team and unable to defend its championship. In the end Tiger played through his misery and shot three respectable 72s, which tied him for eighteenth.

ESPN chose to televise the NCAA Championships in response to the interest Woods had generated in amateur and college golf, but Tiger was unable to summon a full measure of his talent. He shot rounds of 73, 72, 70 and 71, and tied for fifth, three strokes behind the winner, Chip Spratlin of Auburn, while Stanford tied Oklahoma State for the team championship, necessitating a playoff. Stanford lost on the first extra hole.

Although Tiger had been named a first team All-American and his stroke average of 71.3 was the best in Stanford history, he fell short of the NCAA player-of-the-year honors, which went to Georgia Tech's Stewart Cink. The tournament was over and he had failed to achieve one of his few remaining goals as an amateur, to win the NCAA as Nicklaus had done. After his freshman year, he would have three more chances to do so, provided he stayed in school.

Though Tiger was still an amateur, his summer schedule involved more professional tournaments than amateur events, including the U.S., British, and Scottish Opens, and the Motorola Western Open. His failure in the NCAA notwithstanding, he had already proven his mettle against amateur players. They were his peers only in a superficial sense; in reality, he was without equal on the amateur level, and he set the standard used by others to measure their own games. When he went to the driving range at a college or amateur tournament, other players stopped to watch him hit balls. He was simply longer and more consistent than his contemporaries, and he had a greater variety of shots coupled with the ability to execute them under pressure. While other college players were still developing their games, Tiger was working at refining his.

To prepare himself for the pro level, he knew that he first needed to increase his level of competition. Toward that end, he intended to play almost exclusively against professionals in the summer of 1995. He began with the U.S. Open, a more democratic tournament than the invitation-only Masters. The

Open, as its name implies, is open to anyone capable of qualifying.

That summer, the Open was played at Shinnecock Hills Golf Club, a historic links course in Southampton, Long Island, New York. Nearly a hundred years earlier, in 1896, the second U.S. Open had been played on the same course. It is a difficult track in part because of the manner in which the U.S. Golf Association sets up its Open courses—with narrow fairways, high, thick rough, and fast greens. It can also be adversely affected by the prevailing ocean winds.

Tiger went there with the intention of winning, an unrealistic goal by any standards other than his own. "Why go to a tournament if you are not going to go there to win?" he said. "That's the way I have always been, and that's the way I'll always be. This tournament is no different. I am going to go out, play my game, focus on what I have to do, and hopefully my score will be lower than everyone else's."

He arrived in Southampton with rust on his game. The week before the tournament he had had final exams at Stanford, and hitting the books had been an inadequate substitute for hitting the ball. He made it to the practice range only twice that week, and felt that his game was not at the level it had been by the end of the previous summer. This happened every year: school restricted his ability to practice, reducing his effectiveness at the outset of any summer. He had to make up for lost time; he arrived in Southampton on Sunday and played a practice round at Shinnecock Hills Monday morning; in the afternoon he played eighteen holes with his father and the television personality Maury Povich at nearby National Country Club.

As the tournament approached, he also had to face the inevitable questions about his ethnicity. At the Open, he sought to answer them once and for all, by issuing a formal statement to the media:

The purpose of this statement is to explain my heritage for the benefit of members of the media, who may be seeing me play for the first time. It is the final and only comment I will make regarding the issue. My parents have taught me to always be proud of my ethnic background. Please rest assured that is, and will be, the case . . . The various media have portrayed me as African-American, sometimes Asian. In fact, I am both.

Yes, I am the product of two great cultures . . . On my father's side I am African-American, on my mother's side I am Thai . . . I feel very fortunate, and equally proud, to be both African-American and Asian!

The critical and fundamental point is that ethnic background and/or composition should not make a difference. It does not make a difference to me. The bottom line is that I am an American and proud of it!

That is who I am and what I am. Now, with your cooperation, I hope I can just be a golfer and a human being.

By his reckoning, he was just an ordinary golfer. His ability to appraise his own game honestly and to contrast it with that of individuals who earned their livings from the sport reinforced what he already knew. His game was not yet on a par with those of the defending champion Ernie Els or British Open champion Nick Price, his two playing partners for the first two rounds. "Let me put it to you this way," he said, contemplating his competition. "If I mis-hit a shot, I'm beaning the gallery and if they mis-hit a shot they're just catching the green twenty feet away from the pin. Or if I mis-hit a drive, I'm in the hay and they're out on the first cut of the rough."

At the Open, the driver is more often a foe than a friend. And while length is more important than accuracy on the wide fairways at Augusta, the opposite holds true at the Open. Its courses generally feature narrow fairways bordered by the most penal rough in golf. "You don't have a whole lot of room for error," Woods said, "and since I can hit my 1-iron around 260 or 270 (yards), I really don't need a driver that often. I feel I can play my 1-iron all day and be in the fairway. That is very important at the U.S. Open."

In his first U.S. Open round, Woods bogeyed four of the first seven holes. Then he holed a twelve-foot birdie putt at the eighth hole, a thirty-foot birdie putt with a dramatic right-to-left break at the ninth hole, and a two-foot birdie putt at the tenth hole to get back to one-over par, a score that thrust his name onto a professional leader board for the first time in his career. But his round slipped from him when he double-bogeyed the par-4 fourteenth hole by hitting his drive far left and into an unplayable lie, resulting in a penalty stroke. He finished with a 74.

Tiger learned from the round that course management is critical in the U.S. Open, that the conservative shot is more often the best one. "You can't go for broke," he said. "Nick Price is a perfect example. He played very conservatively, within himself, and he made a few long putts and shot a low number."

Analyzing Tiger's game, Price saw Tiger's high number only as a product of his youth and inexperience. He also saw the vast potential. "I can't see where he gets all his power from, but the ball just takes off like a rocket," Price said. "He outdrove me three times today by about fifty yards, and I'm in the top ten or fifteen in driving distance (on the PGA Tour). He's one of the few I've ever seen who's got a normal looking golf swing and hits the ball as far as John Daly. All he's got to do is just learn to play the game, maybe have a little more strategy. He made a couple of mistakes out there, but he certainly doesn't play like a nineteen-year-old. He made some mental mistakes. Hitting the wrong clubs. It seemed like he shot for the pin a lot today. The more U.S. Opens you play, the more you learn you take only a few opportunities to shoot at the pins."

Woods's lack of preparedness was evident; in the second round, he continued to spray his tee shots, with or without the driver. On the third hole, he pulled a 1-iron tee shot left and into the tall fescue grass. He had no other option but to attempt to hack his ball back to the fairway with a wedge, but the club-head got tangled in the fescue. Something had to give, and his wrist volunteered.

"When I came down, it kind of bent my wrist forward and something tweaked in it," he said. "It was a ligament. I sprained it and kept on trying to play with it, but it progressively got worse and weaker. I really couldn't make a grip on the club and I couldn't really swing. I hit another drive left on five and was in the same kind of grass. I tried to hit my sixty-degree wedge and really hurt it (his wrist). I hit my drive on six and that was it. I couldn't hold onto the club with normal grip pressure."

After his tee shot at six, he walked off the course, withdrawing with an injury that further contributed to the fragility charges. In a seven-month span, he had had not only arthroscopic knee surgery and a back spasm, but a strained rotator cuff, food poisoning, and now an injured wrist. His father was unconcerned, attributing the injuries to his son's youth. Tiger was a tall, skinny teenager who had not yet developed physically. Earl asserted that over time he would gain weight and strength, and not break down so readily.

Woods, in all likelihood, was not going to make the cut anyway. After parring the first hole, he bogeyed the next four holes and was eight-over par through twenty-three holes. The thirty-sixth hole cut was six-over par. "I'm kind of bummed out," he said afterward. "I felt I was playing good enough to make the cut. But that's what happens when you hit the ball in the long grass."

The injury sustained at the Open forced him to withdraw from the Northeast Amateur the following week. He went home to recuperate and to begin preparing for the Scottish Open at Carnoustie, a European Tour event he had entered on a sponsor's exemption. It was played in July, a week before the British Open, and he went to accustom himself to the time change and to gain a comfort level with Scottish links courses. Woods became an instant aficionado of links golf, which provided him with the opportunity to tap into his creative aptitude. The American game has largely evolved into one played in the air; approach shots are aimed at pins, and the backspin on the ball, in combination with soft greens, enables the ball to stop almost instantly. By contrast, golf in Great Britain is played on hard, fast courses that reward a quality ground game and a player's ability to bounce the ball onto the green. The greens on these courses tend to reject shots that land on them from the air.

On the practice tee at Carnoustie, Woods picked out a white pole two hundred yards away and began hitting shots at and around it. Then he attempted to hit it with long bump-and-run shots. "He was playing, just playing," Earl Woods said. "First time I've seen him do that in a long time. He was like a puppy out there."

Woods was in contention through thirty-six holes of the Scottish Open, but closed poorly and finished seventeen shots behind the winner, Wayne Riley. But the Scottish Open was only a preliminary event for Tiger. Woods's primary concern was the British Open, which was held on the Old Course in St. Andrews—the ancient university town and the birthplace of golf. St. Andrews is a traditional Scottish links course on the gray, rocky shores of St. Andrews Bay and the North Sea.

At St. Andrews, Woods was reunited with a man who had become his friend, Gary Player, another legend of modern golf who recognized Woods's limitless potential. "When a pretty woman comes into the room, it doesn't take long to notice her," Player said. "The first time I ever saw Arnold Palmer I said, 'there's a star.' The first time I saw Nicklaus, I said, 'superstar.' Same thing with Ernie Els, and I feel the same way about Tiger Woods. As long as he maintains his attitude, he's got it. He is a superstar on the horizon."

Or potentially "the greatest sportsman of all time," Woods's father, Earl, allegedly said, according to a British tabloid that had published a story on Woods during Open week. British oddsmakers suspected the coronation was not imminent and set the odds on Woods winning the British Open at 250 to 1.

Tiger's play at the outset justified the odds. His British Open debut began with a par, then went south when he triple-bogeyed the second hole and wound up shooting a two-over par 74. He recovered with a 71 in the second round and made the cut for the second time in three major championships.

"I'm liking (St. Andrews) more and more," he said with an unbridled enthusiasm that indicated that, unlike many American pros, he would relish the opportunity to travel to the British Isles each summer to play in the Open. "It's the nuances I like most. There are a lot of options around the greens. That's why I play golf, for the creativity. You learn new things every round. I saw bunkers today I hadn't seen before."

Tiger was a nonfactor in the tournament, shooting 72 in the third round and, when the winds came up on Sunday, his slight frame swaying in the gusts, a 78. He finished at seven-over par 295 and tied for sixty-eighth, but "overall it's been an awesome experience," Woods said, "I can't get over the fact that you see buildings and walls that were built in the 1400's, and they're still there. You don't see that in L.A."

*   *   *

The U.S. Amateur in Newport, Rhode Island, was the focal point of his summer, but Woods arrived there having failed to win a tournament in the ten months since the Jerry Pate Invitational at Shoal Creek the previous October. This was the longest such span since he began winning junior tournaments as a young boy.

"The tough part is that every time he plays in a tournament, no matter what it is, he's expected to win," Butch Harmon said. "No one is going to win every time out. As he's gotten better, I think he's feeling a little of the pressure. But he's a much better player than he was a year ago. He's grown much more consistent. He knows more about what he's trying to do. A glowing deficiency, the inability to control the distance of his iron shots, kept him from contending at Augusta. He's worked hard at it since. When I took him on (in 1993), I looked at it as a three year project. He's well ahead of that schedule. I'm very happy with his progress."

His winless streak notwithstanding, Tiger had made a seamless transition to the next level. He had played in five professional events in 1995, and he'd made the cut in four of them: the Masters and the Western, Scottish, and British Opens. Given his inexperience and the inability to properly prepare, he knew he could not realistically have expected much more from his game at that point.

"I've improved so much in the last year," Tiger said. "My scores aren't showing it because I'm not playing in the same kind of tournaments. I've moved up a few levels, so it's hard to compare. I've made every cut except the U.S. Open. Before, I couldn't sniff a cut. It's been very frustrating that I haven't won, but look at the tournaments I've played in. I've played in majors. They're taught to win. Plus, I've never played well during school, because I'm not focusing on golf, I'm focusing on school. The only time I play well is the summer." But because he made nearly every cut, he was "pretty happy" with his over-all performance.

Now toward the end of the summer his game was fine-tuned when he arrived at the Newport Country Club in blue-blood New England. He had continued to gain length off the tee, a frightening development. A few months earlier, his tee shots on the practice tee at Big Canyon Country Club in Newport Beach, California, began clearing the high fence at the far end of the range, reaching the home of a resident who failed to appreciate Woods's prowess with a driver. When the shouting subsided, Woods realized he would have to tee the ball lower to keep it on a lower trajectory in order for it to bound harmlessly off the net.

The course at the Newport Country Club is a links course that abuts the Atlantic Ocean and is watered only by nature; it does not have an irrigation system and, like the Scottish links courses, it relies on rainfall to sustain the grass. Near the end of a dry, hot summer, Newport Country Club was playing hard and fast, and Tiger's tee shots seemed to roll endlessly.

Tiger's mission at Newport was to match history and to trump the Golden Bear. Only eight players had ever won the U.S. Amateur in consecutive years, Bobby Jones among them. Even more important, Nicklaus had never won two consecu-tively. But Tiger was also attempting to win a USGA event in five consecutive years, a feat that only Bobby Jones had bet-tered.

His first round of medal play in Newport was at Wanumeton-omy Golf and Country Club. He shot a two-under par 68 that was at least a stroke higher than it should have been. He missed a tap-in putt from two feet at the third hole.

"Two feet, heck," his caddie Jay Brunza said. "More like twelve inches."

"I rushed it," Woods explained, "and shut down the blade at impact."

More mistakes were in the offing the following day at Newport Country Club, where he shot a five-over par 75 that barely enabled him to finish among the top sixty-four, and advance to match play. "It was a rough day," Woods said. "I didn't hit the ball well and I didn't putt well. I'm extremely disappointed. I don't know what went wrong. But I should get it squared away in fifteen minutes of practice."

Once match play began, Woods was able to settle into a pattern of steady, often extraordinary, golf. Here in a town synonymous with the America's Cup, Woods worked the breeze as artfully as a yachtsman. He displayed an assortment of shots designed for compatibility with the wind and dispensed of his first five opponents without once trailing. Only one of the five even made it to the eighteenth hole: Mark Plummer, a dowdy liquor salesman and the antithesis of Newport's old-money aristocracy. Plummer, forty-three, featured a bushy red mustache and an eyesore of a swing certain to elicit sympathy strokes from unsuspecting opponents, whose wallets would be invariably lighter at the end of the day. He was aware that his unorthodox swing failed to measure up to Woods's polished game.

"He's got more tournament experience in one summer than I've had in my life," Plummer said of Tiger. "He's playing a caliber of golf I know only from sitting in my lounge chair in front of the television."

Yet Plummer had reached the semifinal of the U.S. Amateur Championship and was one victory from dismantling the varied pieces of his swing (one that "only a mother could love," NBC broadcaster Johnny Miller said), packing them up and taking them and his rumpled self to Augusta National for the Masters. He was a deceptively strong player who resembled a golfer only on a scorecard. He was an eight-time Maine Amateur champion and a two-time New England Amateur champion who failed in two attempts to join the PGA Tour.

Plummer featured an uncanny ability to make par from obscure locations. By virtue of seven one-putt greens through thirteen holes, he and Woods went to the fourteenth tee even. Plummer lost the next two holes with bogeys, but won the sixteenth hole and was only down by one going to the seventeenth. "When I won sixteen I got to thinking, hey, everything else has gone right this week," Plummer said. "I thought maybe something was going to happen."

After they halved the seventeenth hole, Plummer's improbable opportunity to win vanished when he hit an errant tee shot at eighteen. "I played as hard as I could play," he said. "It was just a dream, really. It's something I never expected. It's amazing to me, even to get in a position this afternoon with a chance to beat Tiger." Especially in front of his friends who had made the trek from Maine. "It was a big thrill for me. To play the defending champion and the number one amateur in the world and to get to the eighteenth hole, I'm probably the happiest loser you've ever looked at."

Tiger was equally appreciative of his opponent. "He didn't have the prettiest swing in the world," Woods said, "but he kind of got the job done. He hit the ball in places you shouldn't hit it, but he made the putts. He had a style all his own. He had a fabulous short game. He made every putt he looked at."

In the thirty-six-hole final, Woods played George Marucci Jr., better known as Buddy. He was also forty-three, an investment consultant, owner of a Mercedes-Benz dealership, and a member at Merion, Pine Valley, and Seminole, a gilded trio of prestigious clubs in Pennsylvania, New Jersey, and Florida. Marucci had an easy manner and made a lasting impression on Tiger, who at Christmas received a gift from Marucci, a golf shirt from Pine Valley. Yet, on a golf course, Marucci was no one's

Buddy and he cherished the opportunity to thwart Tiger's Amateur defense.

"Candidly, if I have a chance to win I'll get nervous because of what it means," Marucci said. "I've been playing golf since I was six or seven. This is the event I've looked to do well in for thirty-five years. I've waited all my life to get to this point. I never dreamed I'd get this far. My strategy will be pretty much the same. I'm just going to try to play the golf course. Tiger undoubtedly is the best amateur player in the country. I'm going to try not to let him dictate play because he's so powerful."

Suddenly, for the first time all week, Woods fell behind. Through twelve holes, he was three holes down, a deficit he reduced to one by the lunch break. Six holes into the afternoon match, Woods took the lead, but only momentarily. He watched stoically, waiting for the inevitable collapse that did not seem to be materializing as Marucci followed with a series of remarkable clutch shots: a chip shot holed for birdie at the eighth hole (the twenty-sixth of the match) which evened the match, a fifteen-foot par putt at nine, a ten-foot birdie putt at ten, and an eight-foot birdie putt at eleven. "I expected that from him," Woods said. "Every mid-am [career amateur] I played—Sean Knapp, Mark Plummer, and Buddy—all those guys may have hit the ball awry, but they all got up and down (to save par from off the green) from everywhere."

Woods regained the lead on the thirteenth hole when Marucci finally failed to save par. He increased the lead to two holes with three to play when he made a fifteen-foot, downhill birdie putt at the fifteenth hole. When Tiger bogeyed the seventeenth hole, the lead was one again, sending the match down to the final hole, the par-4 eighteenth.

Marucci hit first and his tee shot came to rest in the first cut of the right rough. Woods followed with a perfect 2-iron tee shot to the middle of the fairway. Marucci then hit his approach shot onto the green, twenty feet right of the pin, applying pressure on Tiger, who had 140 yards to an elevated green.

The next shot—the defining shot of the championship—had taken root in April, when Augusta National exposed Tiger's inability to control the distances of his short-iron shots. When he returned to Stanford after the Masters, he became obsessed with fixing the problem. "He worked nonstop on distance control," his Stanford teammate Jake Poe said. "He caught a lot of flack at the Masters about not being able to control the distance of his irons. It was like, 'Tiger Woods hits it far, but he's out of control.' He was hitting his 9-iron 170 yards. So he came back and shortened his swing, knocked it down to three quarters, really worked on distance control. That's what he thought he needed to do to take it to the next level. He sat on the range and hit 9-irons 120, 130 yards, toning it down."

Now, with the championship within reach, he stood on the eighteenth fairway at Newport and pondered the shot. He decided to punch an 8-iron, a shot he had worked on indefatigably in practice and was now going to test under enormous pressure, with the pinnacle of amateur golf at stake. He calibrated the shot to travel exactly 140 yards. The ball hit beyond the hole, then spun back toward the pin. He struck it with such precision that when it finally came to rest it had gone only eighteen inches farther than the distance he had determined it should travel.

When Marucci missed his birdie putt, he conceded Woods's putt and the match, a 2-up victory for Tiger. Moments later Woods and his father embraced on the green, year five of the USGA ritual.

"I figured if I could get it on the green I might make it," Marucci said. "I give him credit. He stood up there and knocked it right up next to the hole. He hit a spectacular shot. It's the sign of a true champion."

Once the stakes were factored in, it became arguably the best shot of Woods's life. "That was the fun of the whole day for me," Butch Harmon said. "To do it for all the marbles was remarkable. Four months ago, he could not have conceived that shot."

Tiger called the shot a punch-draw. The objective of the punch was to control the trajectory, the key to controlling the distance. "Actually it wasn't a draw," he said. "I hit it straight and let the wind bring it toward the hole. I've had trouble controlling the distance on my iron shots. I've spent hours and hours on the range learning how to do it, and it paid off."

The reward was substantial: a second consecutive U.S. Amateur victory earned him return trips to the Masters, the U.S. Open, and the British Open, as well as an opportunity to win an unprecedented third straight Amateur the following year. The relentless media again asked Tiger to assess his place in golf history, a question he now faced regularly as his legend grew. He replied with his characteristic reticence: "My place in history, I don't really care about that. Hey, I'm still a kid. I'm only nineteen."

Too young, even, to share in the celebratory champagne his father drank from the Havemeyer Trophy as a toast to his own considerable contributions over the years. At one point during his son's afternoon round, Earl had been off on another part of the course alongside a vacant fairway. He wore headphones through which classical jazz played, muffling the roar of the distant crowd that cheered his son. Momentarily oblivious to the excitement nearby, he was balanced on his shooting stick and snoring softly. This impromptu nap was a direct result of Tiger's development into the best amateur golfer in the world. Nineteen years of commitment to the growth of his son had rendered Earl bone weary. It was sufficient now that he was with Tiger in spirit; his constant presence at his son's side was no longer required. He had prepared Tiger, the boy, to conquer the golf world, and it was not necessary that he accompany Tiger, the man, who was now on the cusp of doing so.

Earl's relationship with Tiger had begun to resemble that of two best friends more than that of father and son. His role in his son's career was changing. They still discussed strategy prior to each tournament, but Earl was training Tiger to be more independent. At tournament sites, Tiger was the boss; he decided what time to leave for the course in the morning or how long he would practice after a round. When the U.S. Golf Association sent out an entry form for one of its events, Earl no longer automatically filled it out and returned it; he waited for instructions from Tiger.

Earl no longer felt compelled to watch every shot, and Tiger was no longer compelled to search out his father in the crowd. Earl viewed much of Tiger's match with Marucci on a press-room television set, making his way outdoors only to watch the thirty-sixth, and final, hole. He was at greenside when Tiger stood over his triumphant shot in the fairway. Moments later, when Marucci conceded Woods the eighteen-inch putt and the match, Earl was there for the traditional victory embrace.

Nearly as impressive as Woods's execution from the fairway at the eighteenth was the prediction of it by NBC's Johnny Miller. "I wouldn't be surprised if he hit it a foot [from the hole]," Miller said as Woods stood over his ball in the eighteenth fairway. He was off by only six inches.

Through the years, Miller had developed a keen appreciation for Woods's skills, and in the aftermath of the Amateur he predicted that Tiger would eventually win as many as five green jackets at Augusta. It was, in effect, the start of a trend. In the wake of the U.S. Amateur, overwhelmed by his abilities, the media was beginning to ignore Woods's ethnicity. Whether he was an African American or an Asian American had begun to matter less than his status as an accomplished golfer destined for greatness.

As expected, Tiger was named to the U.S. team for the prestigious Walker Cup Matches in Wales, his last event before returning to Stanford to begin his sophomore year. Meanwhile, speculation among those in the media and golf industry was gathering momentum; would he turn pro after his sophomore year or would he remain in school until he earned his degree, as he so adamantly insisted? He offered few hints, even to his Stanford teammates.

His only unfulfilled goal as an amateur was to win the NCAA Championship, and he had another opportunity to do so the following June. And since no one had won the U.S. Amateur three years in succession, he was determined to remain an amateur at least until after the Amateur Championship the following summer in Portland.

Beyond that, he was uncertain. He was satisfied with his progress, but acknowledged that he had not yet proven conclusively that his game had reached a level that would enable him to compete and win on the PGA Tour. He also loved school for both the academics and social activity. Who could tell what the future held for him?

A Buddha, perhaps? When Tiger was home for the Christmas holiday, his mother took him to the Thai Buddhist temple in Los Angeles for a prayer. As an afterthought, she asked a Buddha there to predict what 1996 had in store for Tiger. "The Buddha said in the beginning of the year, he be just like a fish," Kultida said, "but later on in the year he be like a dragon."

Tiger paid little heed to the Buddha, for he was not interested in impersonating a dragon. His mind-set, as unwavering as ever, was on a Bear. It was on Jack Nicklaus.

chapter eight

They strolled down the first fairway at Augusta National, side by side by side: three chapters of golf history—two of them complete, and the third containing numerous blank pages for the spectacular tales to be written there over time. Arnold Palmer and Jack Nicklaus flanked Tiger Woods, three of a kind playing before a full house. They were together for a practice round in preparation for the 1996 Masters, and their audience was ten deep. This was Tiger's second visit.

Woods, only twenty and an amateur, was the guest of honor; Nicklaus and Palmer were there seeking to judge for themselves the breadth of Tiger's talent. They were indelibly impressed. "Both Arnold and I agree that you could take my Masters [six] and his Masters [four] and add them together, and this kid should win more than that," Nicklaus told the media after the round. "This kid is the most fundamentally sound golfer I've ever seen at any age. I don't know if he's ready to win yet or not, but he will be the favorite here for the next twenty years. If he isn't, there's something wrong."

It was a heady endorsement from a man who over the years had transformed Augusta National into his personal stage, winning the Masters six times. But his own act had run its course, and he saw in Woods a talent destined to move to the fore at Augusta. Woods was so long that Nicklaus conceded it made his own game "look puny." At the fifteenth hole, 500 yards long and wide enough to accommodate a driver, Tiger chose a 3-wood—out of deference to Nicklaus and Palmer, in an attempt not to further show them up with his extraordinary length.

Some in the media felt that Nicklaus was burdening Woods with unrealistic expectations, not realizing that he too was swept up in Tigermania. He was acknowledging that he had witnessed a golf game that was on a fast track to heights that only he had attained. Early in the threesome's practice round, Nicklaus was unable to contain his enthusiasm for Tiger's game, and he delivered much the same speech privately to him as he did later to the media.

Gary Player was also playing that day just ahead of Woods's group. At one point during the round, he pointed backwards and alerted the gallery, "Go look at that fellow playing behind me. That's golf's next superstar."

Whether he already deserved that title was the question of the moment. When Tiger returned to Augusta for the 1996 Masters, expectations had risen dramatically. The press resumed their speculation about whether his amateur career was coming to an end, about whether it would conclude with his defense of the U.S. Amateur in August. The irony of Tiger's career is that he has always arrived at the next level ahead of schedule, even though he has been content to take his time and proceed only when he was ready. This patience dates to the young boy who dominated his age group, but resisted the pressure to play against older boys so he could remain with friends. It continued through his years at Western High, when he chose to forgo U.S. Open qualifying to attend his high school graduation. Aside from his propensity for fast food, he has required none of the instant gratification that is the hallmark of his generation.

Of the possibility of turning pro, Tiger said only "that when it's time, it's time, and right now it's not the time." Always attuned to his strengths and weaknesses, he was realistic and cautious about pushing himself to a level at which he was not yet comfortable. As to whether his game had been sufficiently honed to compete week in and week out on the PGA Tour, Woods said, "When I have my A game, I'd have to say I can make a run with them. But I know that, overall, these guys would beat me more times than not. My game is not as good as it should be or could be. Or will be, I hope. I saw a lot of shots I didn't know how to hit. There's also the thinking. These guys are course strategists. With the way they set up courses on tour, you have to be strategically intelligent. My course management is good for the level I'm playing, but it's not tour caliber."

Yet even as he was in the process of taking his skills to a level that would enable him to compete professionally, the rest of the golf world seemed bent on persuading him that his time had arrived, and that it would introduce itself at the Masters. A more pressing question than whether he would turn pro later in the year was whether, as a twenty-year-old amateur, he was capable of weighing in at Augusta, not as a curiosity, but as a contender.

"He's so much better, number one, physically, as a golfer," Harmon said when asked about Woods's improvement. "His golf swing is so much better, so much sounder. The ability to control the distance of his shots is a thousand times better. And I think he's more mature, more grown up. He's just a better golfer. He could contend. I don't know if it's going to happen, but he's good enough."

Earl Woods was bracing himself for a breakthrough performance. He recalled the Pacific Northwest Amateur nearly two years earlier, when Tiger had pronounced himself at his peak and then won the thirty-six-hole final, 11 and 10. Now, the week before the Masters, Tiger phoned home from Stanford, and the first words he spoke to his father were strikingly familiar.

"Pop, I'm ready," Woods said.

He himself came into the tournament expecting to contend, especially having improved his control over the distance of his iron shots. "Overall, my game has improved to the point where I'm able to shoot more consistent scores. My college golf has shown that. And my driving is much better. The pressure internally is still there. Externally, it's different, because I know what to expect around here. Going through that learning experience was kind of difficult at times, because not only did I have to try and play, but I had to get used to all the hysteria that goes on around here. That will help. And I'm pleased to say I haven't got lost in the clubhouse like I did last year."

On Monday and Tuesday Tiger played practice rounds with Norman, who joined the chorus of those who were convinced the future had arrived. "He's gotten better," said Norman, who had not played a round with Tiger in about ten months. "He's longer. His iron play is more under control. He is exceptionally long. I think he's longer than John Daly. He flights the ball so good. He's just going to become better and better. I wouldn't be surprised to see somebody like Tiger there at the end, unless he gets swept up in the situation after shooting a good score."

They were joined on Tuesday by Fred Couples and Raymond Floyd, each of them passing along advice to Tiger on how to maneuver around Augusta National. "They have a lot of knowledge and they're willing to share their knowledge," Tiger said, "and that's very nice of them. These guys know the course like the back of their hands." He found their tips invaluable in his effort to overcome his lack of experience at Augusta.

The tournament began according to tradition, with Gene Sarazen, ninety-four, joining Sam Snead and Byron Nelson, to hit the ceremonial first shots. Afterward, Sarazen was asked about Woods and expressed bewilderment over the fuss. "When I was twenty [in 1922]," Sarazen said, "I won the U.S. Open *and* the PGA Championship."

En route to Augusta National's resident haberdasher, in his attempt to collect the first of the eleven green jackets Nicklaus had predicted he'd win, Tiger tripped over the golf world's lofty expectations. He opened with a round of three-over par 75.

"He shot 75 today?" Nicklaus said. "I don't know how."

From the fairway in, he was off the mark. He had hit all fourteen fairways, but he'd missed eight greens and needed thirty-three putts to complete his round.

"I think I hit some good shots," Woods said. "I'm pleased with my play overall. But I didn't putt very well. It's disappointing. I'm still in there, but I've got to have a good round tomorrow. You never know. It's a four-round tournament."

It was in fact a two-round tournament for Woods, whose scores were worse than the year before. He shot a second straight 75 and missed the cut. His round included an eight-foot downhill putt on the eleventh green. Once he started the ball rolling, he was unable to stop it. It gathered momentum and tumbled off the green.

"It's disappointing," he said. "Then again, I played much better than I did last year. The conditions are a lot tougher. I putted off the green at eleven, and it wasn't because of a bad putt, either. The wind hit it and knocked it off the green. But I didn't really putt well. I was not hitting my line and I had a tough time reading them, and that added up to pretty poor putting. You can learn forever here. Jack's still learning. Greg Norman got some tips from Raymond Floyd the other day. I'm still learning.

"It's like Jack Nicklaus told me, you have to be patient here. Jack said he missed the cut his first year, and had eight three-putts. It took him five years to win it. There are only two ways to learn this course. You have to listen to the guys who have played it, and you have to go through the diabolical experience of playing it."

When Tiger flew back to California, he left his disappointment behind. He never pouted over failure, and whatever the degree of his anger, it dissipated quickly. Missing the cut at Augusta only strengthened his determination to come back in 1997 and beyond, so that he could carve a niche for himself in Masters' lore. He wanted to make good on the promise his father had made to the Augusta caddies a year earlier, the promise of a Technicolor green jacket.

In the meantime, he had an economics paper due on Wednesday.

His poor performance at the Masters did nothing to alter the consensus that sometime soon he would be a force at Augusta National, a feeling that for others might heighten the temptation to move on to professional golf. Had it done so for Tiger? Even his Stanford teammates were unable to determine whether he intended to turn pro before he graduated.

"He never talked about his future," teammate Eri Crum said. "The most I'd ask him was, 'What's your feeling about turning pro?' That was always the big question on the team, whether he was going to turn pro or if he was going to stay the four years. He would always give you sort of an indecisive answer. He always sort of avoided the question. He told me he wasn't going to turn pro unless something dramatic happened at the British Open. There was always a sense of surprise to me on what would happen, because he would never share with me anything about his future."

His standard answer was this: "I'm not turning pro until I feel like I'm going to go out there and make a difference."

Earl had even considered taking out an insurance policy from Lloyd's of London as a hedge against an injury that might end his son's career before he had had a chance to cash in. But he decided against it. He did not feel it was warranted, because of the non-injury nature of golf. And he knew that Tiger was physically maturing and not likely to suffer a career-threatening injury.

Moreover, purchasing an insurance policy might invite the charge that money was an issue in Tiger's career, Earl said. "None of this is about money. If it was about money, Tiger would have turned pro a long time ago and I'd be a rich man, and we'd be laughing all the way to the bank."

The college season was winding down and Woods, as usual, had been a dominant player. He'd won six of ten tournaments, and the remaining dominoes were in place. The Pacific 10 Championships were scheduled to be played on his home course, the Big Canyon Country Club in Newport Beach, where he was an honorary member. The NCAA West Regionals were to be held at the Stanford Golf Course, and the NCAA Championships were scheduled for the Honors Course at Ooltewah, Tennessee, where Woods had made his U.S. Amateur debut five years earlier.

In the days leading to the Pacific 10 Championships, a prominent member at Big Canyon, one of the most exclusive clubs in California, asked a newspaperman to refrain from publicizing the tournament. "We (the club) don't want any publicity," he said, echoing a consensus among members.

The request was as absurd as it was too late. The members ought to have considered that before they had extended their invitation to the Pacific 10, which featured the most prominent player in NCAA history, one it was especially eager to showcase. Tiger did not do his part to stifle publicity either: thirty-six holes were played the first day, and he played them in eighteen-under par. It was a day that ranks among the most remarkable in golf history at any level. He equaled an NCAA record and set Pacific 10 and course records with an eleven-under par 61 in the morning round. In the afternoon he shot a seven-under par 65. In the morning he had birdied six of the first seven holes en route to a front nine of 30. Each of his scores bettered the previous course record of 66, one Tiger had tied months before without informing anyone. (He had concluded that it was not worth noting unless he set the record.)

The temperature at Big Canyon was in the 90s that day, and players on the college level are required to carry their own bags. Woods's coach, Wally Goodwin, was struck dumb by Woods's performance in the stifling Southern California heat. "On a hot day, carrying his own bag, he shot 61 in the first round and then rested fifteen minutes and had to go out and do it all over again, and he shoots 65," Goodwin said, shaking his head.

By the end of the first day, Tiger had opened a fourteen-stroke lead. The following day, several hundred people were on hand, most of whom would never have been allowed on the premises of this exclusive country club had it not been for the Pacific 10 Championships. Woods played the final two rounds in even par and concluded the tournament at eighteen-under par 270, eclipsing Corey Pavin's conference record of 273. He won by fourteen strokes, the margin he had opened on the first day of play.

At the NCAA West Regionals, Woods maintained his torrid pace, playing fifty-four holes in eight-under par 205 at the Stanford Golf Course and winning by six shots to advance to the NCAA Championships in Tennessee.

An NCAA victory was still the one void on his amateur record. With or without a victory in the NCAA, his amateur legacy was complete, but that was not enough for him. Jack Nicklaus won the NCAA Championship, as had many of the more notable names in golf from the past forty years: Hale Irwin, Ben Crenshaw, Tom Kite, Curtis Strange, and Phil Mickelson. Moreover, Nicklaus was one of only two players to have completed the NCAA–U.S. Amateur double in the same year, a goal Tiger wanted to match.

He opened the tournament with a 69, one stroke behind Pat Perez of Arizona State, who had tied an Honors Course record with a 68. The following day, Perez's name was erased from the Honors Course record book only a few hours after it had been entered. Woods broke the course record, shooting a five-under par 67 that gave him a three-stroke lead. He increased his lead to nine strokes with a 69 in the third round, and even though he stumbled in the final round, shooting an 80, he was still able to win the tournament by four strokes. From Ooltewah, Tiger traveled to the Memorial—a PGA Tour event in Dublin, Ohio—to receive the Jack Nicklaus Trophy, awarded to the college player of the year. PGA Tour pro Fuzzy Zoeller, who was competing there, spotted Tiger and jokingly commented, "Nice three rounds, kid."

Tiger's NCAA performance was in fact a solid four-round effort that illuminated the gap in skill level between him and the other college golfers. He knew that, should he continue to play college golf as a Stanford junior, he ran the risk of losing interest, which might do him more harm than good. He had now cleared his final amateur hurdle, winning the NCAA Championship. Aside from an opportunity to win an unprecedented third straight U.S. Amateur and to complete the NCAA–Amateur double as Nicklaus had once done, was there anything more for him to accomplish on the college level? Tiger had not played on an NCAA Championship team, but to contend a team requires five top-flight golfers, and the Stanford golf program seemed to lack the necessary depth. Even with Woods, Stanford was not likely to win the NCAA Championship in either 1997 or 1998.

Once he had won the NCAA individual title, Tiger became intrigued with the prospect of turning pro later that summer. But he was pragmatic about his capacity for succeeding immediately as a pro. He was concerned that his game had not yet progressed to a level that would permit him to be consistently competitive as a professional. Before he made the break from amateur golf, he needed proof that he would be making the right decision—the kind of proof that would only come from playing well in a professional event.

Countering this argument was his sense that his game was now too polished to derive any additional benefit from college and amateur golf. These levels of play generally failed to challenge him, and so he had begun to feel that he had outgrown them. Jack Nicklaus and many others sensed this, and at the Memorial Nicklaus asked him whether he intended to turn pro. But Tiger still insisted that he was returning to Stanford in the fall unless he accomplished something dramatic over the summer.

Tiger had only two tournaments in which to produce the requisite drama, the U.S. Open and the British Open. Inasmuch as no amateur since Bobby Jones had won either tournament, the prospect was remote that another amateur—even one as precocious as Woods—would ever win them again.

The U.S. Open was held at the Oakland Hills Country Club in Birmingham, Michigan, on a long, hard, straightforward golf course. Tiger was paired with Corey Pavin and John Daly in the first two rounds, but even though Pavin was the defending champion, he was on the undercard in this group. The main event featured the two heaviest hitters in golf.

"John will probably outdrive me all day because the course is so soft," Woods said. "Because of his long swing, it lends itself to a higher launch angle, which means he's going to carry the ball a lot farther than I do. He can carry it past me on the fly at any given time with his driver. But on a firm fairway, I hit a lower ball flight and I can turn it over a little bit. When my ball hits hot, it will roll."

The first opportunity to flex their muscles came at the par-5 second hole, each of them hitting a driver. Tiger's drive landed in a puddle, which killed its ability to roll, but it still measured 322 yards. Daly followed with a drive of 339 yards.

Tiger concluded the hole with a tap-in birdie that put him under par for the first time in a major championship. By the fifth hole, this kind of play made the story shift from Woods vs. Daly to Woods vs. the field. At five, he holed a sixty-yard shot with his lob wedge for birdie to go two-under par, placing him on the leader board. Another tap-in birdie at the par-5 twelfth hole gave him a share of the lead.

For a moment, it was as though the future had arrived on cue, at the national championship, the U.S. Open. But even with Woods's skill at focusing on his task, a minor glitch derailed him. Or, as they say in golf circles, the wheels came off. The fourteenth hole was the beginning of a disastrous string of holes. His second shot trickled only an inch or two off the green, but a drain on the green blocked his line and removed the putter from his hands. Tiger was required to chip to clear the drain, and his execution was faulty, the ball winding up ten feet right of the hole. He missed his par putt and made his first bogey of the day.

"I was cruising along," he explained afterward, "hitting fairways and greens. I was very solid, very confident. But that drain threw me off a little bit. I had a nice putt at it. Unfortunately, I had to chip it because there was the drain there, and I hit a bad chip."

His game continued to unravel as he pulled his tee shot into thick rough at the fifteenth hole. He was able to extricate it with enough strength to reach the front fringe of the green, but a poor chip and three putts gave him a double bogey. At the sixteenth hole, he lost his second shot right, and it caromed off a bank and into a pond. He took a drop 170 yards from the hole and hit a sand wedge. The ball hit pin high left of the hole, then spun back off the green and into the pond again. He wound up with a quadruple-bogey eight.

"I thought I hit a good shot," he said, referring to the shot that followed his first drop. "I was playing it left of the hole, attempting to use the slope to bring it back toward the hole. I hit it right where I was aiming, right at my spot. Unfortunately, it didn't stick."

He bogeyed the seventeenth and eighteenth holes, too. Playing the last five holes in nine-over par, he shot a six-over par 76.

"Things like that happen," Daly said. "They're going to happen to all of us. It's happened to me a hundred times. But he's tough. He's very mature for a twenty-year-old. When I was twenty I was drunk all the time."

Was another force at work, other than the rub of the green? When Tiger had taken the lead, he noticed that security within the ropes was reinforced. No one explained to him why this was happening. Meanwhile, rumors had spread through the press tent that a threat had been made on his life. The commander of the police detail for the U.S. Open, however, denied that a threat had been received. "We've heard nothing," Sgt. Steve Berg of the Birmingham Township Police Department said. "The three officers walking with Tiger Woods heard nothing, and there have been no telephone calls."

Earl Woods was not satisfied with this explanation or with everyone's denial that security had been increased. "All I know is that Tiger says, yes, he feels like something happened, because security was reinforced with his group shortly after he took the lead. This is speculation, but somebody evidently didn't like the idea he was leading the Open. The USGA has said nothing to me, but something caused a whole bunch of security to be out there that wasn't there before."

Tiger did not let the incident distract him the next day. Heeding his father's long-standing advice that he should not worry about things over which he has no control, he recovered his lost momentum and shot a one-under par 69 in the second round, one of only twenty sub-par rounds played that day. For the first time in the Open, he made the cut. At this point, he also dropped his first public hint that he was considering turning professional. A third consecutive victory in the Amateur could conceivably be the springboard to a pro career, he said. "It all depends on how I feel, how my game has progressed, whether I'm ready or not. You know, it's a big decision, because once I do it there's no turning back. It's going to take me awhile to sit down and make sure I make the right decision for me."

The following two days weren't likely to hasten his move to turn pro. He finished with two unspectacular rounds, a 77 and a 72, and tied for eighty-second. When he returned home, he accepted an invitation to appear on the *Tonight Show* with Jay Leno. Though he once said that he was opposed to doing talk shows because, "that's not me," he had matured to a point where he felt more comfortable in front of audiences, and he accepted the invitation.

When he sat down opposite Leno, the host displayed a photograph of Woods as a baby wearing a diaper and holding a golf club.

"You don't see many pros in diapers," Leno said grinning.

"I should have had one on at the Open," Woods replied.

If Tiger's U.S. Open performance failed to persuade him that he was prepared for professional golf, he was determined that the British Open would do so. He encountered a minor setback when he began the tournament at Royal Lytham and St. Annes with a four-over par 75, the third straight dismal opening round for Woods in a major championship. But the following day he rebounded with a five-under par 66.

"Everything clicked," Earl Woods said, "the things I'd been trying to tell him about his approach to the game, to abhor a bogey, that distance isn't a factor unless strategically used. It's like dancing. You're doing the mechanics, and then the music starts and it flows."

Woods closed the British Open with a pair of one-under par 70s, giving him three straight sub-par rounds. He finished in a tie for twenty-second and was awarded the Silver Medal, presented to the low amateur in the Open. This consolation prize was of dubious value to Tiger, however. "Heck," he said, "I was looking for the Claret Jug. That's what I came here for."

More significantly, he had traveled there to establish in his own mind that his game was polished enough to compete at the highest levels of golf. That he had succeeded was a reward of greater value to him than the Silver Medal. He felt that he was making significant progress.

Tiger's performance in the British Open sparked renewed interest in the golf world and the media as to whether Woods would be returning to school. He continued to insist that he would return to Stanford in the fall, but in the meantime he was consulting with a wide variety of confidants on whether the time was right to turn pro that summer. PGA Tour pros and close friends were among them, though his Stanford coach, Wally Goodwin, who believed Tiger was returning to school, was not. The opinion that perhaps carried more weight with Woods than any other belonged to his teacher, Butch Harmon. He was the person Tiger turned to, concerned about whether he had a swing capable of holding up under the pressure applied by the best players in the world.

When it came down to his decision, Harmon said, "I've told Tiger and his parents, when they ask me, that physically his game is at a level where he can play the pro tour. He has such tremendous talent. I personally think he could go play the PGA Tour right now. His game is ready. I don't think I've seen anyone with this talent since Nicklaus."

These were the words Tiger had been waiting to hear.

The swing is the fingerprint of the golfer; no two are alike. Jack Nicklaus's swing differed dramatically from Lee Trevino's swing, but they were similar in one important regard: they were repetitive, each swing identical to the next, the key to consistency.

Tiger has similarly grooved his swing, so that from shot to shot, or tournament to tournament, there is virtually no variation. He also has what Nicklaus called the most fundamentally sound swing he has ever seen, a conclusion that prominent teaching professional Peter Kostis agreed with. "I'm of the belief that if you have a good grip, a good setup, good alignment and balance, the golf swing by and large takes care of itself," Kostis said. "Tiger's basic fundamentals are almost flawless. As a result his golf swing works very consistently, and the only variable that I see in his golf swing has to do with rhythm and tempo. But that's the case with most tournament players."

When the repetitive nature of Tiger's swing is merged with sound fundamentals and the suppleness of a lean twenty-year-old, the result is a potentially lethal mix of extraordinary length and accuracy.

Though Tiger weighs in at 160 pounds, give or take a "Quarter-pounder," he is a heavyweight by anyone's standards, and it is apparent by the tales of the tape measure: the first hole at Brown Deer Park Golf Club, a drive of 336 yards; the fifteenth hole at Augusta National, 500 yards, driver, 9-iron; the twelfth hole at Oakland Hills, driver, 5-iron; the fifteenth hole at the

TPC at Summerlin in Las Vegas, 315 yards, 3-wood into the back bunker.

When it is said that Tiger is long on potential, the emphasis should be on the word "long." "Guys in the locker room are often talking about his length, and some of the places he hits it, usually prefaced by, 'You won't believe this but . . . ,' " Brad Faxon wrote in *Golf World* magazine.

At the U.S. Open, Faxon engaged in a debate with U.S. Senior Open champion Tom Weiskopf, who argued that Woods's power was in part a product of technology, that modern equipment has shortened golf courses and Woods has simply exploited technology more than others. Surely he doesn't hit it farther than Nicklaus did in his prime, Weiskopf noted. Yes he does, Faxon countered adamantly, citing Woods's clubhead speed.

"It's always been there," Woods said, explaining his power. "I've always been long, naturally, even when I was very little. I was always long for my age. I've had enormous hip speed and shoulder rotation, and it's just been natural. It's like asking Ken Griffey Jr. how he hits these 500-foot home runs. He doesn't know, he just does it. I'm the same way. I've been blessed with natural speed, and I've worked on my mechanics to help control that and then harness that speed into more consistent play."

He has also had growth spurts, each one adding distance to his drives. "I remember a time when I grew a half inch in two weeks," he recalled. "And I gained about twenty yards, just because my swing arc changed just a little bit. And when I got stronger, that changed my game a lot. Ever since I went to college and I got stronger, I got a little bit longer."

His tempo, balance, and footwork are perfect. At the top of his swing, the club is just short of parallel to the ground. He generates enormous clubhead speed with a swing that has not

ROBERT WALKER/USGA

ROBERT WALKER/USGA

Tiger at the U.S. Junior Amateur in 1992.

Tiger embracing his father after his victory at the U.S. Amateur in 1994.

Tiger on the third tee of the 1996 Augusta Masters, flanked by enthusiastic fans.

Tiger during the 1996 U.S. Open at Oakland Hills.

Tiger's record-breaking victory at the U.S. Amateur in 1996.

Tiger with the winner's trophy at the 1996 Las Vegas Invitational.

Tiger's victory at Disney World, 1996.

Two Tigers and a mouse, Disney World, 1996.

Tiger at the Skins Game, 1996.

Tiger clowning with Fred Couples at the Skins Game.

Frustration after hitting a poor chip shot.

Tiger swings at Pebble Beach, 1997.

been unnaturally altered for that purpose—in the manner of John Daly, who has the longest backswing in golf. As a result, Woods is exceedingly more accurate than Daly and nearly as long.

Kostis pointed out that a swing is a three-lever system: the golf club, the left arm, and the area from the sternum to the left shoulder. "Genetically, wide-shouldered people have a bigger lever from the sternum to the left shoulder," Kostis said. "Tiger has tremendously wide shoulders. He's blessed genetically with the opportunity to create more power. The whole key to developing plenty of clubhead speed is to be able to crank that left shoulder around your spine as fast as possible. It comes from the legs and hips, and his leg and hip speed is incredible."

Tiger's swing is the product of inherent talent and the three primary teachers in his life. Rudy Duran, now the director of golf at Chalk Mountain in Atascadero, California, was the first. Tiger was four when he began working with Duran, who understood that with a client that age little more was required of him than assuring that Tiger be fundamentally sound, that his grip and posture and set-up be correct. John Anselmo, now retired and living in Huntington Beach, California, took over from Duran when Woods was ten. When Earl Woods recognized that his son's swing only needed refinement to take him to the next level, he sought the assistance of a pro's pro, Butch Harmon, a teacher who taught professionals. Tiger's favorite player had been Greg Norman, and Earl liked what Harmon had done for Norman's swing. In 1993, the day after Tiger was eliminated in the second round of match play in the U.S. Amateur at Champions Golf Club in Houston, Earl took him to see Harmon at Lochinvar Country Club, where he is the director of golf.

"At the time he just wanted me to take a look at him and make some recommendations," Harmon said. "He was this skinny kid with this long, loose golf swing with absolutely no control over where the ball was going. He hit it as hard as he could, found it, and hit it again. He hit the ball a mile. But he was already an incredibly hard worker and he was like a sponge, soaking up advice from everyone, from me, from other players."

Tiger studies the game meticulously, and his approach over the years has been to borrow the qualities of a variety of players. Now that he makes his home in Orlando, Florida, he is a frequent visitor to the Golf Channel headquarters library, where he sits viewing videotape by the hour.

"I've never tried to emulate one person," Tiger said. "Every person has faults. I've tried to adopt the best attributes of many people. I've always studied great players. They were great for a reason. I like to find out why they were great. I used to love to watch Tom Watson putt, Trevino hit little wedges, or Nicklaus hit long irons. I would watch how they did it and why. More important, I like to study their decision-making on the golf course. I've tried to pick fifty players and combine the best of them, and to make one super player."

When Harmon took over Tiger's nurturing, it was as though the Hope diamond had been entrusted to him and he had been asked to polish it. Had he done nothing, it would still sparkle. Any tinkering and he ran the risk of harming the swing. But Harmon chose not to view it that way. The firstborn son of Claude Harmon, the 1948 Masters champion, Butch is a strong-willed teacher who takes great pride in his work. He laboriously studies videotape of his clients, and he goes about his work with diligence. It was said that he was the only man working for Norman who was willing to stand up to him, and who got away with it. Clients who do not heed his advice are certain to hear about it later.

He had a client in Woods who was advanced beyond his years. "His mechanics were basically perfect," Harmon said. "His grip and posture were perfect." Tiger's alignment and ball position required no adjusting either.

With such a solid foundation to work from, Harmon deduced that refining Woods's swing and maximizing its effect was a three-year project. The two developed a long-distance relationship, with Woods either at home in Cypress or in school at Stanford, and Harmon in Houston. Tiger sent videotape of his swing for Harmon to analyze, and they spoke frequently on the phone.

Harmon's first order of business was to widen Woods's stance. "Anytime you generate that much clubhead speed, you have to have a good foundation," Harmon said. The narrower stance promoted a steeper swing arc, requiring that he use his hands more to get the clubface square at impact. As long as he already was, the long backswing, fast hands, and poor footwork deprived him of additional distance, and cost him accuracy as well. Tiger's shots were often crooked, a fault he frequently overcame with his ability to manufacture remarkable recovery shots. But to fully capitalize on his length advantage, he required greater accuracy off the tee.

"I've tried to gear his swing down some, shorten it so that he can control the flight of his ball more, take something off his shots under pressure," Harmon said.

By widening his stance, Tiger swings with a wider arc, which has improved his footwork and enabled him to rely less on his hands, thereby increasing his consistency in squaring the clubface at impact.

"It gives the appearance of a shorter swing, but it's actually longer because of the arc," Harmon said. "He's very quiet with his lower body, and with such a wide arc it's almost like cracking a whip." He noted that in all his years of teaching he has never seen greater clubhead speed than that produced by Woods. Yet Woods remains in perfect balance and his swing is almost effortless. "That's the beauty of Tiger," Harmon said. "He's under control doing it. He drives the ball beautifully. When he first came to me, he said he just aimed down the middle and hit it as hard as he could, and if he missed the fairway, he figured he'd have hit it far enough that he could still reach the green. Now, he actually hits the ball farther, with less effort."

Harmon has taught him to reduce the speed of his swing to seventy-five to eighty-five percent of capacity, which gives him greater control. The only time he should attempt to reach one hundred percent, Harmon said, is when the situation requires that he take the risk to gain an additional thirty or forty yards.

For Tiger, this has meant any par 5. A goal Harmon established for Woods is that he hit his drive in the fairway more frequently on par 5s. Harmon had observed that on these holes in particular Tiger still had the mind-set of a college player, who thinks he has to hit it farther so as to reach the green in two shots—in the process sacrificing accuracy. Tiger was not required to muscle a drive to reach most par 5s in two.

Except on par 5s, Tiger was aware that swinging at full speed impaired his accuracy, and for the most part, he throttled back. "I can hit it thirty yards farther, but there's no point because I don't know where it's going."

Some elements of the swing—the balance and tempo—were there from the beginning. But Harmon refined the swing and transformed it into a professional one—a swing without excessive movements, capable of holding up under the pressure of tournament golf at the highest level.

"I knew my swing was a little like Greg's," Woods said. "Butch was successful with him, and I wanted similar changes in my swing. My swing would not have held up over the long haul. He has changed it and refined it. It's better than it's ever been."

He also felt more confident with his iron play. "When I was very little, it used to be a strength of mine, but then as I got older I got a little longer on my swing, got a little too loose. It hurt me a little bit. But now it's becoming my strength again. It's basically taking advantage of good situations where I hit a good drive down there or I'm just in the fairway or something. Now I feel like I can attack because I have the distance control and the accuracy with irons."

His suppleness enabled him to effortlessly rotate his shoulders until his back was facing the target, while keeping his left heel grounded. His clubhead speed, meanwhile, was generated in large measure by the quickness in his hips, imperceptible to the untrained eye. "He has incredible lower-body speed," Harmon said.

"Tiger's swing is technically as good as or better than Norman's," Johnny Miller wrote in *Golf World*. "And I thought Norman's swing was the best on tour. I like Tiger's whole game—chipping, putting, sand play, everything. Add that to his Nolan Ryan-like quality, his 128 miles per hour clubhead speed, and he's something special."

Woods learned from an early age the value of a preshot routine. To this day, Earl Woods knows Tiger's preputt routine so well that, once Tiger has addressed the ball, Earl can close his eyes and do play-by-play commentary, concluding at the precise moment that Tiger's putter makes contact with the ball.

"He takes one practice stroke, another, and another," Earl says. "He looks at his target, he looks at the ball, he looks at the target again, he looks at the ball. Impact."

Tiger seems to have an innate ability to create shots in the manner of Seve Ballesteros, who has an uncanny talent for extricating himself from trouble. He once admitted that he even looks forward to hitting his tee shot into the woods, thereby enabling him to devise a recovery shot. He has already grown to love Scottish links golf, where the game is played as much on the ground as in the air. Targets are reached by bouncing the ball toward them rather than flying the ball at them. This satisfies Tiger's appetite for innovation, which some feel is genius at work.

"Tiger, how'd you do that?" Earl would ask him after his son had executed such a shot.

"I don't know," Tiger replied. "I just did."

At Stanford his teammates tried to get inside Woods's head to see whether they might learn from his mental approach. "If I asked a direct question, like how he was hitting the ball low, he would always have a technical answer," Eri Crum said. "I was trying to figure out what he was thinking when he hit the ball that way. He'd just always answer with so much confidence, as though it was a weird question or something, because it was so easy for him. 'What do you mean what am I thinking? I know the ball is going that way. I don't even have to think twice about it.' "

Tiger is a range rat; he can entertain himself for hours on the practice tee, running through every club in his bag and working on a variety of shots until he has mastered them.

"He was serious at practice," Stanford teammate Jake Poe said. "There's a saying, you go down to the range, you've got some guys who work on their swing and slap at range balls all day, and you've got other guys practicing golf, practicing shots. That's what he'd do, practice shots on the range."

"He knew his golf swing so well," another Stanford player, Conrad Ray, recalled. "He could go out to the range and hit twenty balls and fix whatever he was trying to fix. Guys on the team, we'll go out and hit balls and we'll *find* something to work on. Instead, Tiger knew what he did wrong the previous day or during the previous round and he'd go out there and fix it. That's what separates the good pros and the college players. I think all the guys on our team can hit the shots pretty much, maybe not as consistently, but we can all hit the shots. It's just a matter of knowing what to work on, and working on one thing and knowing your swing."

His talent is a combination of a strong work ethic, a lifetime of exposure to the game, and good coaching. But it might be something more, something indefinable.

"People ask me why he's so good," Conrad Ray said. "There's a lot of pros that will tell you because his golf swing is so good, or he's got the greatest short game. I personally think he's got a gift that most people don't have, like a Michael Jordan, those types of people. There's a lot of it that can't be explained. He's just a natural. He's got this gift to play great golf."

But it was a gift that had been continuously refined over the years, his swing evolving into something with no discernible flaws. It had earned Butch Harmon's stamp of approval—an important piece of a puzzle that, once assembled, would make Tiger's decision about turning pro an easy one.

chapter ten

On a golf course, Tiger was equipped to block out distractions, to narrow his focus until only the shot at hand was visible to the mind's eye. He would have done well to apply this skill off the course, for as his celebrity grew, so too did the demands of his time—from both the media and the expanding throngs of fans attempting to interact with the new golf hero. He envisioned interviews and autograph requests potentially commanding the bulk of his free time each day.

Studying the game itself, Tiger habitually examined the methods of the greatest players, searching for clues to the secrets that made them great. He took a similar approach for adapting to life in the spotlight by inviting Arnold Palmer to dinner. Palmer, the most popular golfer in history, had set the standard on coping with the masses and the media. He possessed a charisma that enabled him to connect with the public and be responsive to the demands of the media.

The pair met on October 3 at the Silverado Resort in Napa, California during Tiger's sophomore year at Stanford. Palmer was in town to play in the Transamerica, a Senior PGA Tour event. On the ninety-minute drive from Palo Alto to California wine country, Tiger thought about the questions he had for Palmer and anxiously awaited his audience with this distinguished member of golf royalty.

When Tiger arrived, he and Palmer were escorted to a quiet table in a corner. They enjoyed the evening, exchanging tales of golf past and present—the King, as Palmer is known, and his wide-eyed heir to the throne.

"He helped out a lot," Tiger said later, "because we were in comparable positions. I was headed toward where he used to be. When he first burst onto the scene, when he had all the hoopla and all the fame and the rush that he brought to the game, that's kind of the direction I was headed. I wanted to learn from him what he did, so I wouldn't make mistakes."

When their dinner and conversation concluded, the check came and Palmer reached for it. He paid the bill, as any multi-millionaire, even the infamously frugal Palmer, would do when dining with a cash-poor college student.

When news of the dinner meeting was mentioned in a Chicago newspaper, sirens simultaneously sounded at the headquarters of the National Collegiate Athletic Association and in the offices of the athletic department at Stanford University. A student athlete had accepted a free dinner: man the battle stations. Stanford officials immediately confronted Tiger and interrogated him on the matter of the bill. When he informed them that Palmer had indeed paid, the university notified the NCAA and Tiger was suspended, pending an investigation.

The problem was that, according to NCAA regulations, student athletes were not allowed to receive benefits based on their athletic status or reputation. Woods thought that the ruling bordered on the paranoid, and he felt both confused and angry. He had simply been having dinner with a friend, a man he had known for several years. "I felt like I hadn't done anything wrong," Woods said, noting that all he'd done was dine with a friend from whom he sought advice. "For that I'm told I'm going to be declared ineligible."

Stanford officials, assuming that Tiger would understand their actions, misgauged the depth of his anger and remained oblivious to his growing concern that if he were to so much as sneeze, an NCAA official monitoring him from behind a potted palm might say, "Bless you." His growing stature had made him a magnet for scrutiny, and nobody wanted to hurt his eligibility.

The violation was determined to have been minor and inadvertent, and in the end the NCAA allowed the suspension to last only a day. Stanford coach Wally Goodwin, meanwhile, attempted to trivialize the matter. "It's all cleared up," he said. "There's no suspension."

The fact was that there had indeed been a suspension, Tiger said, and the matter had not been cleared to his satisfaction. When he was en route to El Paso, Texas, for a college tournament, he was not even certain he'd be eligible to compete. He had been informed by officials that he was suspended, but had not yet been told that the suspension was lifted.

Several weeks earlier T-shirts had been distributed by employees in the Stanford athletic offices. Silk-screened onto them was this message: "If it's fair and reasonable, it must be an NCAA violation."

Tiger surely would have concurred. His mood in El Paso was that of a man who has just duck-hooked his drive out of bounds. It irritated and angered him to have his motives questioned. When he phoned home he told his parents, as though he was ready to renounce amateur golf, "I don't need this." Many wondered if the incident might expedite his ascent to professional golf. "I don't think it will," he said, "but you never know. It's annoying."

The suspension lasted only a day, but Woods's anger was more enduring. Woods sent Palmer a check for twenty-five dollars to reimburse him for the cost of his meal, bringing the issue to a close and creating a valuable item of memorabilia: a check with Woods's signature on the front and Palmer's signature on the back.

Shortly before Christmas Tiger and his Stanford teammates attended an informal dinner at Sam's Grill in San Francisco to raise funds for the East Palo Alto Junior Golf organization, an affair that raised enough money to send twelve impoverished kids from the Palo Alto area to the Stanford Golf Camp. Coach Goodwin had brought along a few items to auction, but in the course of the evening he suggested to Tiger that they auction the Palmer check. Without giving it a second thought, Tiger agreed. The check fetched a top bid of five thousand dollars.

When Earl learned of the auction, he was incensed and his anger was directed at Goodwin for showing a lack of judgment by not discussing the matter beforehand. He felt that the check should have remained the property of the Woodses. Despite his initial approval, Tiger had to agree with his father.

This episode further contributed to Tiger's disenchantment with college golf. The entire Palmer incident was in fact the beginning of the end of his college career. It was part of a series of events that moved him closer to making the leap into professional golf. "The first time I started thinking about turning pro was after the Arnold Palmer decision," Woods admitted. He already had been suspended once before, in the aftermath of the 1995 Masters. While he was in Augusta, he had written diaries on his experiences there for *Golf World* and *Golfweek* magazines, and though he was not remunerated for his work, he was found guilty of an NCAA violation, and Stanford suspended him for a day. The diaries had been branded as the promotion of a commercial publication, and Stanford had been forced to declare him ineligible. But because of the obvious inadvertence of the violation, there was no penalty and his eligibility was restored twenty-four hours later.

Too often for Tiger, Stanford and the NCAA had questions that contributed to his perception that the scrutiny was oppressive as well as unfair. At the Masters, for instance, Tiger had struggled to control the distance of his short-iron shots, frequently hitting the ball over the greens. At his father's urging, he elected to replace his Mizuno irons, 6 through pitching wedge, with Cobra irons that belonged to Harmon. Stanford, concerned that he might have received free equipment that had not been issued through the university, an NCAA requirement, asked Tiger to account for the source of the clubs.

At the same tournament, Greg Norman, a spokesman for Maxfli golf balls, suggested to Tiger that he try Maxflis instead of the Titleist balls provided by the university. Tiger agreed to test them in a round, but was again confronted by the university.

By then, Earl Woods was also exasperated with Stanford's scrutiny of his son. "If you look at this situation objectively, this is the perfect opportunity for Tiger to say, 'kiss my yin yang,' and leave school," Earl said. "Everybody would understand. They (the NCAA and Stanford) just went too far. The irony is that Tiger genuinely likes Stanford and wants to go to school. If he left, he would be in line to make no less than twenty-five million dollars. Tiger really doesn't need the NCAA and he doesn't need Stanford. He could leave and be infinitely better off, except that he wants to go to school."

Earl took responsibility for helping his son wade through the regulations, and he painstakingly attempted to acquaint himself with the cumbersome NCAA rulebook. When Tiger was given an honorary membership at Big Canyon Country Club several years earlier, Earl had consulted with the United States Golf Association and the NCAA to ensure that no rules had been violated that might jeopardize either Woods's amateur standing or future NCAA eligibility. He was determined to have Tiger play by the rules, but he was beginning to suspect that the rules were too inflexible to accommodate basic common sense.

In spite of his disenchantment with the bureaucracy of college sports, Tiger had fallen in love with Stanford and the college experience. He'd had so much fun beyond the classroom walls that he felt he had squeezed three years of social activity into two. He enjoyed his schoolwork and being able to take classes as unique as Portuguese Cultural Perspectives. But the NCAA's meticulous scrutiny was slowly eroding the pleasure. "This is not fair," Kultida Woods protested, "not for a kid who is trying to set an example for kids who want to follow him, by staying in school. They're trying to drive him out of school."

Even if he was privately contemplating leaving school, it still angered him when the uninformed began to state unequivocally that he would turn pro in the summer of 1996. ABC Sports's Brent Musburger on two occasions announced over the air that Woods intended to turn pro. This rankled Tiger, particularly, because at the time he had no such intentions. It was still only one of several options and had not yet become a likelihood. "He knows more about my life than I do," Tiger said. "He's never asked me anything."

Nevertheless, by the spring of 1996, his frustrations with the NCAA converged with the fact that his ability had moved him to a level in college golf where he was devoid of viable competition. He was longer, more accurate, more consistent, more focused, a better putter, and more determined than any of his peers. He won nine of thirteen tournaments his sophomore year, including the Pacific 10 Championship by fourteen strokes and the NCAA Championship by four. He was a man among college boys who occasionally defeated him, but no longer presented enough of a challenge to provide him with the incentive to continue playing at their level.

Still, he had never been in contention in a professional event, nor had he played in one impressively enough to demonstrate that he was ready to take the next step. He was making cuts in professional tournaments with greater frequency, but had not sustained a level of play that enabled him to contend. He had missed the cut at the Masters and though he was briefly tied for the lead in the first round of the Open, he went nine-over par in a five-hole stretch that spelled his demise there. His indecision about turning pro was reinforced by his sense of being in limbo, of hovering between two levels. He knew he was overqualified for one, and wondered if he was qualified for the next.

It was with his sporadic record at the professional level that he arrived at Royal Lytham and St. Annes for the British Open in the summer of 1996. He had missed the cut at the Scottish Open the week before, but this was only a tune-up for the main event, which Tiger had been anxiously anticipating for months. The previous spring he had confided in Stanford teammate Eri Crum that he did not intend to turn pro, "unless something dramatic happens at the British Open." His performance here would dictate his future plans.

At the Masters that spring, Jack Nicklaus had declared that Woods would be the man to beat at Augusta for the next twenty years. Some in the media interpreted his remarks as a calculated effort to construct expectations that could never be met, while at the same time reinforcing his own standing as the greatest player in history. It's just as likely that Nicklaus had genuinely recognized a talent that was potentially the equal of his own. A man often described as condescending and the product of a lifetime of hearing he was without peer, Nicklaus may have been acknowledging that this was no longer the case. He had been witness to a parade of purported "Bear apparents" throughout the years and had finally recognized a viable candidate. And he seemed determined to make certain that Woods's potential would not go unfulfilled. After Tiger opened with a 75 at Royal Lytham and St. Annes, Nicklaus took him aside and gently admonished him for playing his way out of contention on opening day, as he had done at the Masters and the U.S. Open.

"I don't ever want to see you shoot 75 in the first round of a tournament," Nicklaus said. The message was implicit: it is as important to dig down and grind in the first round as it is in the last.

"He gave me a little lecture," Tiger said. "It was kind of neat, that he cares about me that much. I came to understand that to win a major, or any golf tournament, you can't win it on the first day, but you can lose it on the first day. And I lost it on the first day. When you're not playing well, you still need to get in the clubhouse around even par. I learned it the hard way."

The next day Tiger shot 66, the first of three successive sub-par rounds he played, a transformation that did not go unnoticed. "He's as good at his age as Jack [Nicklaus] was," said Michael Bonallack, the secretary of golf's governing body, the Royal and Ancient. "And look at what Jack has done in the game of golf. That's the highest praise I can give anyone, to compare him to Jack Nicklaus."

Woods finished in a tie for twenty-second, marking the first time he had performed, in a professional event, at a level commensurate with his ability.

"The patience level has improved," Harmon said, assessing the reasons behind Wood's resurgence. "I was so upset with him when he got the lead at the U.S. Open and had a few bad holes and disaster struck him. We talked a lot about that at the British Open. He was four-over the first day, then was two-over through five holes on the second day. Then he played the last thirteen holes in seven-under. It was truly the most patience I'd seen him show. It was one of those things I thought was previously lacking. It was a little bit of immaturity—that when something goes wrong, he wanted to get it back right away."

Before the U.S. Amateur, Tiger had one more tournament to play, the prestigious Western Amateur in Benton Harbor, Michigan. He had won the event in 1994 and for the third straight year played well enough over seventy-two holes to be among the sixteen players who advanced to match play. But he lost his first-round match to Terry Noe of Fullerton, California, a former U.S. Junior Amateur champion. At the end of the match, angry and disappointed, Tiger headed for his car with reporters tailing him. "I'm outta here," was his only comment to the media. He was not referring simply to Benton Harbor.

Three years earlier, Woods's lethargic play in a junior tournament in Colorado had been a sign to Earl that his son had outgrown junior golf, and this same attitude had resurfaced at the Western Amateur. "I didn't want to be there," Tiger admitted. He left Benton Harbor and drove to northern Michigan in search of respite from the golf world, and to spend a few days of rest and relaxation with friends. During this time, he considered his options, weighing the advice he had sought and received in recent months.

Some remained cautious about his jumping into professional golf, including his teacher Butch Harmon, who had discussed the situation with Earl and Kultida on numerous occasions. Harmon insisted that, while Tiger's physical abilities had reached the professional level, Tiger lacked the maturity he would need as a professional. He urged Tiger to stay at Stanford. "School is the most fun you'll ever have. If you turn pro, you're going to miss out."

But most of those around Tiger were of the same mind as Curtis Strange, who was perhaps the most outspoken proponent of Woods turning professional. He went public with his opinions during his role as a commentator of ABC Sports's telecast of the British Open. "I've thought he should turn pro the last three, four, five months. He's ready physically. He's mature enough. He has nothing else to prove whatsoever in amateur golf. The quicker he gets out here, the quicker he gets to be the best player in the world. You learn how to play golf out here, you don't do it in the amateur ranks. I personally think the day he gets his card he'll be a top thirty player, and he'll do nothing but improve, with the potential to be the best player in the world some day."

Tiger, meanwhile, had reached a similar conclusion. After he returned home from Michigan, he looked his father in the eye and said simply, "I'm ready, Pop." When pressed by his father to explain his reasoning, he carefully cited his performance at the British Open as well as his success at the collegiate and amateur levels. He stated his case with determination, and it became clear to Earl that Tiger's mind was made up.

They would discuss it in greater detail later, Earl said, but in the meantime he accelerated his own role in Tiger's career. Working behind the scenes with Hughes Norton of the International Management Group, he began mapping out Tiger's future in the event that his decision to turn pro was final.

Earl would later be criticized for orchestrating a professional career for an amateur, implying that in doing so he had compromised Woods's amateur eligibility. This frustrated Earl, who openly wondered why similar inquiries were not made when Phil Mickelson turned pro and had instantly signed contracts reportedly worth six million dollars. Or why no one questioned the fact that Archie Manning had begun to interview agents on behalf of his son, Tennessee's junior quarterback, Peyton Manning, in an attempt to gauge his son's value should he turn pro. Earl saw himself as similar to the father of a student on the threshold of graduating, who assists his son in setting up a job that would await him once he was finished with school. He made sure no rules were breached and no contracts signed. He and Hughes Norton worked on hypothetical agreements only so that they'd be adequately prepared in the event that Woods indeed turned pro in the aftermath of the 1996 Amateur.

Tiger had already made that decision. He would attempt to

defend his U.S. Amateur Championship, then would renounce his amateur standing and make his professional debut in the Greater Milwaukee Open the following week. Even if he lost the Amateur, he intended to turn pro.

In the meantime he had decided that to publicly announce his intentions would be an invitation for distractions. To survive the most grueling week in amateur golf, it was imperative that he maintain his focus, and the announcement would have triggered a media frenzy. Even with his closest friends he only hinted at his decision. As the U.S. Amateur approached, he told a few of his Stanford teammates that if he won he was turning pro. And if he lost?

"Who knows," Jake Poe said. "He wasn't going to lose. He knew he was ready. He'd always said, 'I'll know.' He knew."

The final hurdle was cleared when Earl and Kultida gave their approval to Tiger, but only after he had convinced them that he had made an informed, rational decision to which he was committed, and that he agreed to their one request.

"I want you to finish school because Jack Nicklaus did not finish school," Earl told his son. "Arnold Palmer did not finish school. Curtis Strange did not finish school."

"I promise you, Pop," Tiger replied.

chapter eleven

Life as an amateur golfer and student was relatively simple for Tiger Woods. His most pressing concern was fitting practice around the time-consuming demands of a Stanford education. Financial considerations were nonexistent; his education was paid for by his scholarship, and his mother and father had always been willing to sacrifice to see that his golf needs were met.

This is how it had always been for Tiger. When he was a child, his greens fees were paid by his father. Later, his celebrity was the only currency required to play golf, and it had earned him his honorary membership at the Big Canyon Country Club in Newport Beach, California, where the de facto dress code states that only pants with deep pockets are permitted.

"Do you know," Earl said one day, teasing his son, "that Tiger will never have to pay a greens fee in his life? He probably thinks golf is free. He'd be surprised to learn that the rest of us have to pay." It is unlikely as well that Woods has ever known the cost of a sleeve of golf balls. In this protected environment, money was irrelevant to him; his parents provided the necessary equipment, requiring only that he hit the books with the same passion and purpose as he hit the driver.

Life for Woods was a short par-5 with a wide fairway and an unguarded green, until he arrived in Portland, Oregon, on August 16, 1996, to compete for the last time as an amateur in the United States Amateur Championship. Not only was he leaving the amateur ranks, he was also leaving the working-class existence he had known all his life. The modest, aging two-bedroom tract house where he had grown up in Cypress, stood in stark contrast to what was ahead, an opulent life of expansive estates, luxury automobiles, and corporate jets. "I'm never flying coach again," Tiger said to his father as they sat uncomfortably in the cramped seats of the commercial airliner that took them from Orange County to Portland for the Amateur.

For his part, Earl Woods would never again object to the cost of airline tickets, as he had done for this flight and all those before it. This particular fare had set him back three hundred dollars more than he had intended to pay because he had had to make changes on their nonrefundable tickets. Three weeks earlier, Tiger had phoned Earl to inform him that he had just learned that the U.S. Amateur was starting a day earlier than originally scheduled. Somehow news of the change had eluded Woods, the two-time defending champion, even though the change was a testament to his ability and star power. It had been made to accommodate NBC, which asked that the quarterfinals and semifinals not be played on the same day. This enabled the network to televise an additional round of match play, presumably featuring Tiger as the star attraction, a certain ratings winner.

At the Hillsborough Airport in Oregon, a corporate jet was already standing by for Tiger and his family. The jet was waiting to whisk Tiger off to the rest of his life, which only he and a few others knew was to begin in Milwaukee, Wisconsin, in a matter of days.

Tiger's immediate future had already been meticulously plotted in the war rooms of the International Management Group, and Nike. IMG, the mammoth global sports agency, had won a long and spirited recruiting war that some say began when Woods was barely a teenager. Throughout Tiger's teen years, IMG employed Earl Woods to scout junior golfers, a job viewed by the media and other agents as a cutthroat way for the agency to make a down payment on Tiger's future, though it was also a job for which he clearly was qualified.

Earl zealously defended this arrangement and denied any impropriety. Those who questioned his role with IMG might have wondered from Earl's biting response whether the wrong Woods was called Tiger. Typical of his reactions to such queries was the one given to *Golfweek* magazine: "It irritates me that people would insult my intelligence to think that I would sabotage this young man's career. It's obscene. It's crazy to think a parent would do that. I can work anywhere I want to, and the operative word is 'work.' Nothing given. Work. I understand how the world operates. And if you think you can buy me for a lousy fifty-dollar scouting fee, you are really sick in the mind."

Earl's association with IMG failed to dissuade other suitors, each of whom pondered a sizable commission should they be given the opportunity to negotiate an endorsement contract for a signature line of Tiger woods and irons. In November 1994, Tiger was invited to Palm Desert, California, during the Skins Game to meet with Payne Stewart and Paul Azinger, a pair of PGA Tour stars represented by Leader Enterprises, Inc. "I don't know anything about it," Azinger replied when he was asked by a reporter what the purpose of the meeting was. "But I'd be more than happy to talk with him. It's going to be a tough row to hoe for him. The expectations that are going to be heaped on Tiger Woods will be the strongest test of what a man can bear. I'd be happy to share with him." The meeting was eventually scrapped when the Woods family concluded that an agent's recruiting pitch was behind the invitation. Another agent approached Earl at the Amateur and cut to the quick: a fire sale representation, half off whatever commission percentage IMG charged, as well as an interest in an equipment manufacturing company.

In helping Tiger select an agent, Earl's primary consideration was finding one with vast international experience. He sought to align his son with an agency capable of capitalizing on Tiger's Asian heritage and his expanding global appeal. Headquartered in Cleveland, but with offices in Tokyo and London as well, IMG seemed best situated to help Tiger launch a career destined to make him an international superstar.

Though no agreement would be signed until Tiger officially turned pro, the decision to retain IMG had been made by Earl and Tiger earlier in the summer of 1996. Several weeks before the U.S. Amateur, IMG had prepared press kits, including a release announcing that Woods was turning pro. The itinerary IMG devised for Woods listed a news conference scheduled for Wednesday, August 28, at Niketown in Chicago, the day before Woods's professional debut in the Greater Milwaukee Open and three days after the final of the U.S. Amateur.

Acting on instructions from the Woodses, IMG already had negotiated a pair of lucrative endorsement contracts for Tiger, notably a five-year, $40 million deal with Nike, which intended to trumpet its coup at the Niketown news conference. Earl, meanwhile, had surreptitiously requested and received sponsors' exemptions on Tiger's behalf into seven PGA Tour events—the maximum allowed to those who are not members of the PGA Tour—for the following two months. The public only knew about two of them, one to the Greater Milwaukee Open and the other to the Quad City Classic, both tournaments in which Tiger had originally intended to compete as an amateur prior to returning to Stanford at the end of September for his junior year.

By now Tiger had no intention of returning to school that fall. It was perhaps symbolic that at the Amateur he was the only player in the field who eschewed short pants in favor of long the entire week, despite stifling humidity and temperatures that reached one hundred degrees. It was a conscious decision by Woods, who had felt that he had outgrown shorts. He had made the decision to become a professional and had simultaneously determined that it was time he dress like one. It was a subtle hint to those who watched that he was in the process of a metamorphosis.

From the first time he had picked up a club, he had an uncanny ability to close his mind to whatever lay ahead, enabling him to hone in on the task at hand. On the golf course he could ride the momentum of his own hot hand to a landslide victory, yet blithely dismiss an opponent's momentum as an aberration that wouldn't last long. The upshot has been an innate ability to play one hole, one shot at a time, without looking ahead to a trophy presentation.

Now, for the first time, he was contemplating the future, a virtual invitation to disaster in sports. A cluttered mind so diminishes the focus required in a game of such precision that, during tournament week, Woods avoids any beverages that contain caffeine, a hedge against overstimulating the nervous system. But now on the verge of stepping into the professional arena, he was required to look beyond his golf game. He was forced to turn his attention to decisions on which tens of millions of dollars were at stake. To accommodate his new financial status, he was in the process of establishing a corporation, ETW, and installing himself as chairman and his father as president. He was also arranging to purchase a townhouse in the upscale Isleworth community of Orlando, Florida, where he had intended to move for several years. The urgency of the move was precipitated by the voracious appetite of the California state income tax, and Florida—with no state income tax—was a haven for professional golfers. Meanwhile, Nike was promising to make him the "Air apparent" to Michael Jordan.

Virtually overnight, his life had been radically transformed. One day, his most pressing concern was whether to have pizza or burgers for dinner. The next day, he was pondering contract offers, real estate transactions, and tax shelters.

The man most interested in securing a piece of Tiger's future was Phil Knight, the CEO of Nike, who made the short drive each day from Nike headquarters in Beaverton, Oregon, to Pumpkin Ridge to dutifully follow Woods as he played in the Amateur. On one particularly torrid day early in the week, the eccentric multibillionaire arrived attired in a plantation hat, a light yellow suit, a black T-shirt, and a pair of multihued sneakers that clashed not only with the rest of his wardrobe, but with the very definition of fashion. Knight stood out like a pair of Reeboks in a town that subsists in large measure on Nike's presence, fueling the widespread speculation that Woods himself was attempting to quell—that he intended to turn professional at the conclusion of the Amateur.

When he stepped to the first tee on the Ghost Creek Course at Pumpkin Ridge, Tiger had more than just the future to contend with. He also had to negotiate the present, a field of 311 other players, each of them hoping they would be the chosen one summoned to redirect the course of history.

Also vying for Woods's attention was the past: the legend of Bobby Jones, who was generally regarded as the greatest amateur ever to play the game. Jones, who had never played professionally, had retired from competitive golf at twenty-eight after winning five U.S. Amateur titles. But he had never won more than two in a row, and now, in Oregon in 1996, Woods was attempting to win an unprecedented third straight.

This was the tournament toward which Tiger had geared his entire year. He had already played in the Masters, the U.S. Open, and the British Open, a gilded triumvirate with enough collective prestige to bust the U.S. Amateur to the rank of club championship in the psyche of anyone other than Tiger Woods. But the U.S. Amateur represented a unique opportunity for

Woods to shape history, the only incentive he has ever needed. Tiger wanted to set records, and no one had ever won three Amateurs consecutively. "The greatest players ever, Nicklaus and Jones, never did this," Woods said. "I like to be unique, to accomplish things that have never been done." To a degree he had already done so, with his three consecutive Junior Amateur championships, followed by consecutive Amateur championships, and his enviable position as the only player ever to have won both of these tournaments. Now, before he turned professional, he had only a single hurdle left, and it carried the visage of Bobby Jones.

To help Tiger avoid the distractions of these various obstacles, Earl had planned for every contingency—mechanical or mental—by bringing along Team Tiger, the group he had assembled years before to help nurture Tiger's development. Team Tiger included his teacher Butch Harmon, and his sports psychologist Jay Brunza. As he had for each of Tiger's five USGA victories, Brunza was enlisted to caddie for Tiger, though he gave way after medal-play-qualifying to Bryon Bell, Tiger's best friend and former teammate on the golf team at Western High School in Anaheim.

If Tiger's focus had been diverted, it was not evident in the two qualifying rounds designed to pare the field to the sixty-four players who would advance to match play. He shot rounds of 69 and 67 on the two courses at Pumpkin Ridge and, much to his surprise, was the medalist. "Am I? Am I really?" he said, raising his eyebrows and expressing amazement. "That wasn't the plan."

In general, he placed no more importance on being the low qualifier than he did on eating nutritious foods. His goal was simply to finish in the top sixty-four and advance to match play. By finishing first, he provided his onlookers with both a glimpse of his raw potential and an insight into how his ability could exceed his own considerable expectations. But winning the medal was a portent of nothing in the Amateur; only once in the previous ten years—Phil Mickelson in 1990—and only three times in the previous fifty-five years, had the medalist gone on to win the tournament.

That night Tiger made his usual pass through the drive-through lane at the McDonald's in nearby North Plains, ordering by rote a Big Mac and fries. En route to the course the following morning, he drove through again, this time ordering an Egg McMuffin. Employees there, recognizing a celebrity in their midst, began documenting Tiger's orders beneath a photograph of him that they had posted adjacent to the drive-through window.

This was indicative of the kind of attention Woods was generating. People came to the U.S. Amateur in record numbers to see the prodigy who had become the most formidable marquee name in golf, the individual capable of saddling even Greg Norman with second billing. The crowds at Pumpkin Ridge were there almost exclusively to follow Tiger, and they were so substantial that from the outset Kultida received special dispensation from the USGA to follow Tiger from inside the gallery ropes, since, on her tiptoes, this diminutive woman can barely see over a pitching wedge. The first time Tiger played in the Masters, she attempted to smuggle in a periscope, a violation of Augusta National's stringent spectator rules. She was caught with the contraband, which was confiscated, and then spent the entire tournament straining to see her son hit shots. If the USGA had not intervened on her behalf at the Amateur, she would have had a similar view of the back of a spectator's shirt.

Tiger's first-round opponent on the Witch Hollow Course was J. D. Manning, a Colorado State senior. Manning's downfall began on the eighth hole, where Woods holed a forty-foot, downhill putt by deliberately blading the ball with his sand wedge from the fringe. Either genius or luck was at work, but from Manning's standpoint, the case was closed. It was genius.

"The guy hits a great shot at eight," Manning said with unbridled admiration. "There's nothing you can do about it. It's a little disheartening. It took the wind out of my sails. He's got as much game as anybody has ever seen. He's the best player I've ever played with." The shot provided a psychological advantage for Tiger, who went on to defeat Manning, 3 and 2.

That night, Woods, Brunza, and Bell went to see the film, *Tin Cup,* and on their way home drove to Waverley Country Club in Portland, where Woods had won the last of his three U.S. Junior Amateurs. They walked quietly to the fairway bunker at the eighteenth hole, where in the Junior final three years earlier Woods had played one of the most dramatic shots of his life. Needing a birdie to tie the match, Woods had hit a forty-yard bunker shot to within eight feet of a hole nestled on a small plateau at the back of the green, and then holed the putt.

Three years later, in the fading light of a late summer day in the Northwest, the threesome stood in the fairway at Waverley and solemnly recalled that decisive shot. Golfers draw confidence from visualizing quality shots from their past, and this was the one that inspired Tiger's performance that week. "It was a spontaneous thing that evolved from going to the movie," Brunza said. "It was a positive reverie, a reminiscence that will always be there."

He needed a storehouse of successful shots to tap into for his second-round match with Jerry Courville, a thirty-seven-year-old coordinator for Pitney-Bowes in Milford, Connecticut. Tiger's toughest opponents in previous U.S. Amateurs were generally career amateurs in their late thirties and early forties with two- and three-piece swings ostensibly held together with duct tape. They had wives and kids and jobs, and an uncanny ability to get up and down for par from virtually every imaginable predicament. They tend to frustrate college players, who consistently outdrive them and have more inherent skill, and yet can't seem to shake the veterans when it matters most. Tiger had faced three such players in the Amateur in 1995, including Buddy Marucci, who had been his nemesis in the thirty-six-hole final.

Courville was of a similar vein. He was the reigning U.S. Mid-Amateur Champion, a veteran of the U.S. Open and the Masters, and he wasn't likely to cower in the presence of a man of twenty, however towering his reputation.

Tiger had learned that this kind of opponent was not likely to lose passively, that their years of experience had taught them how to keep grinding until the match was over, unlike many college players, who in a tight spot would quit.

But even tenacious veterans will succumb quietly beneath the weight of a birdie barrage. Tiger had also learned the importance of applying constant pressure on an opponent, and he birdied six of the final nine holes to defeat Courville, 4 and 2. "I wish good luck to anyone playing Tiger this afternoon," Courville said. "If anyone is going to beat him, they are going to have to go pretty low."

The next to try was Charles Howell of Augusta, Georgia, who at seventeen represented Woods's first younger U.S. Amateur opponent. Howell was an exceedingly talented player with a wry sense of humor. On the information sheet each contestant was asked to fill out, Howell had written that he had a superstition: don't walk under moving cars. When Howell had been just a skinny, bespectacled fourteen-year-old with big feet, Earl Woods had taken notice of his ability and declared that if anyone was capable of equaling Tiger's record of three consecutive U.S. Junior Amateur championships, it was Howell. Though he never won the Junior—he lost in the final in 1996—he was a legitimate threat, capable of derailing Woods.

Howell failed to heed his own superstitious advice, however. The moving car, more of a freight train operating at full throttle, was his opponent, and he flattened Howell. The difference in the level of their ability was underscored by the second shot Tiger hit on the 553-yard, par-5 eleventh hole, from 235 yards into the wind. Woods faded a 2-iron to within fifteen feet of the hole. They don't teach that shot at Stanford.

"I didn't lose 10 and 8," Howell said at the conclusion of the match, "so I'm happy. He's awesome. You have to play really well and match him shot for shot, if not better."

Howell lost, 3 and 1, but Tiger, for the first time the senior player in a match, was greatly impressed with the younger player. "He's a lot straighter than I was at seventeen," Woods said. "I was longer, but I could hit it off the map at any given time. He hits it very crisp and very solid."

Tiger himself, that week, was generally hitting it straight, which took the pressure off the rest of his game. Already among the longest hitters in the world, he had tamed his penchant for misdirecting his tee shots, a tribute to his work with Harmon. As he approached the quarter-finals, he was striking the ball with confidence and precision, and he was pleased by his course management, a critical element for succeeding on this type of layout, particularly with the rough growing taller and thicker, and the greens becoming harder and faster as the week progressed.

Although he had advanced to the quarter-finals, Tiger downplayed the suggestion that he was closing in on history. "It's just another match," Woods said. "The only thing that gets tougher is the opponent."

But each day there seemed to be a defining moment that emphatically illustrated the chasm between Woods's ability and that of his opponents. The next player to face this was D.A. Points, a sophomore at Louisiana State University. Against

Points, it came at the 143-yard par-3 twelfth hole. The pin was tucked in the left corner of the green, behind a pond that wraps around the green, guarding the left side and waiting to penalize even the moderately errant shot. It called for the safe play, taking it right of the hole, toward the middle of the green. Tiger instead chose to hit a 9-iron at the pin, and he hit the ball to within six feet of the hole. He then made the birdie putt to go 3 up on Points, who eventually fell, 3 and 2.

This development set up a semifinal match between Woods and his Stanford teammate and friend, Joel Kribel, who had used the opportunity of playing alongside Tiger for a year to help raise the level of his own game. "Tiger pushes me to improve," Kribel said. "Playing with him day in and day out, with him being the best amateur and junior ever, makes you realize how much more work you need to do. I'd never played him in a tournament, but we'd had plenty of little money games. In fact, I probably still owe him a little bit of money."

At Stanford, they ordinarily played for whatever they had in their pockets—change mostly—but here in Oregon the stakes had risen. This time, what Tiger seemed to have in his pocket was the Amateur trophy. He was playing so well that, by the time he met Kribel, victory seemed only a formality. Over the course of a long, hot week, he countered the heat by disposing of his opponents with chilling efficiency, and he was methodically approaching the end of his quest to surpass Bobby Jones.

Kribel loomed as his most prohibitive threat. Over the summer Kribel had won the Pacific Northwest Amateur and the Western Amateur—the two tournaments Woods had won preceding his first U.S. Amateur victory in 1994—so when Kribel arrived in Oregon, he was brimming with confidence.

Unlike other players, Kribel was not awed by Woods. They were friends; they had roomed together on the road, laughed together, played together. When they went to Taco Bell, they vied to see who could eat the most tacos. Against Kribel, Woods was not likely to have a psychological advantage.

As the two friends warmed up on an otherwise empty practice tee, only a few yards separated them, but their stance in relation to the greater golf world was light years apart. Tiger, an amateur who played like a professional, was being monitored by Butch Harmon, a pro's pro, a man who had tutored Greg Norman and Davis Love III. Kribel, meanwhile, worked alone.

The match was more of the same. "Joel talks about the match and says from about the second hole on, Tiger didn't have a word to say to him the rest of the day," Stanford's Conrad Ray said. "Here they are, good friends, but yet Tiger was all business. Stuff like that can get to a guy. He really did everything in his effort to win and he does every time he goes out."

Early in the match, Kribel played as though he were Woods's teacher, determined to give him a lesson. He won the first hole with a birdie and was 2 up through ten holes. Yet he had taken his best shot and had only staggered Woods, who began whittling away at Kribel's lead by the time they reached the eleventh hole. Kribel then bogeyed the thirteenth, sixteenth, and seventeenth holes, and his lone birdie, at fourteen, was bettered by a Woods eagle.

"Tiger took an eight count," Earl said. "He took everything the other guy had, then he knocked him out."

The damage was largely self-inflicted. "I just didn't get it done on the back nine," Kribel said, "and if you open the door for a guy like Tiger Woods you're going to pay for it. And that's what happened."

Tiger continued his pattern of flawless play, and won, 3 and 1. Throughout the match, he did not make a single bogey, running his streak to twenty-six straight holes without one. In 116 holes that week, he was an aggregate twenty-three-under par. As each of Woods's fallen opponents had done, Kribel could only marvel at what he had seen.

"To win two in a row is just phenomenal," Kribel said. "To be playing in the final for three in a row is just unbelievable. If you just have one bad match, that's all it takes. Or if one person gets hot, that's all it takes. You can get beat at any time. To win eighteen straight matches would just be unheard of."

The media sensed that not only was history about to be made, it was being made in a startlingly efficient manner. Was he indeed crafting the climax to his amateur career? Rumors were circulating at a heightened rate among the media that Woods was on the cusp of turning professional. One rumor even had the Nike jet at Hillsborough Airport, waiting to take him and his family to Milwaukee Sunday night.

At his initial news conference at Pumpkin Ridge, Tiger was noncommittal about his future, and, on the eve of the U.S. Amateur final, he continued to deflect questions. He was interested only in talking about his match with Kribel, where he had again shown his ability to excel under pressure—to meld his physical abilities with his mental strength, and get the most out of each.

"Somehow," Woods said, explaining his victory over Kribel, "I dug down deep and didn't really make a mistake on the back nine."

Somehow? This would indicate that chance had entered the equation, but Harmon had seen enough to eliminate chance as a collaborator. "He's such a fierce competitor," Harmon said. "The people he's playing against know he can overpower a golf course, which they can't do. He's proven he's never out of a match. He has that ability in him, the kind of thing all great champions have. He loves the challenge and the head-to-head battle."

By defeating Kribel in the semifinal, Tiger had arrived at the brink of an unprecedented third consecutive Amateur championship. Awaiting him was a college sophomore entrusted with safeguarding the honor of Bobby Jones. His name was Steve

Scott. He was nineteen, from the University of Florida, and he had enlisted his girlfriend, Kristi Hommel, to caddie for him. They frequently stood side by side in the fairway, Kristi massaging Scott's neck, as though they were two against the world. In fact, the crowd found it difficult to resist "young love," as Johnny Miller described it on the NBC telecast, and was not openly rooting against Scott.

Among the better collegiate players, Scott had arrived in the final by disposing of Robert Floyd, son of PGA Tour star Raymond Floyd, and Scott's Florida teammate. Scott had rated his own ability on a par with Tiger when the latter was a seventeen-year-old and winning the last of his three U.S. Junior Amateurs. Scott had opened the Amateur by shooting a 79, which sent him in search of a phone to reserve a seat on an earlier flight back to Gainesville, Florida. Yet he had followed that with a 66, which was more in accord with his ability. This restored his confidence by the time he came face to face with Woods in the final.

His positive attitude was fortified by Tiger's anemic start. Tiger made a double-bogey by hitting a ball into a hazard at the second hole; he then hit two balls into the water at the par-3 fifth. Five holes into the thirty-six-hole final, Scott was 3 up. By the end of the morning round, Scott had a five-hole lead over Woods, who had shot the equivalent of a 76 in the morning round, his worst golf of the week. His swing was out of sync, and he was not holing putts. He knew that if he had putted better, he might be 2 down at worst, and it angered him.

Tiger had a quick lunch, then set out for the practice tee to work with Harmon, who had noticed that his posture was bad on his full swing, as well as on his putting. After correcting the flaws, he was able to breathe easier: "Thank God Butch saw some things."

Back at the Amateur in 1994, when he had been down four

holes to Trip Kuehne midway through the thirty-six-hole final, Earl had taken him aside and delivered a motivational speech that was only a few words long, but carried a resounding impact. "Son," he said, "let the legend grow." Now, two years later, with his son in a similar predicament, Earl was considering what he might say this time. But after a while, he decided not to say anything. He knew his son was now capable of fending for himself.

Tiger delivered his own speech to himself. "I kept telling myself that I've been here before," he said. "The fortunate part was that I had thirty-six holes. I knew I had to make a move early and I did."

Losing was not an option for Tiger, who set about paring the deficit to a level that would give him a realistic opportunity for making a back-nine run at Scott. By the turn, Scott's lead was reduced to one. But Tiger was 2 down with three holes to play, then holed a short birdie putt at sixteen to get within one.

At the seventeenth, Woods was angry with himself for leaving his approach to the green thirty feet from the hole in a crucial situation. Then he calmly holed the putt to tie the match for the first time since the second hole of the morning round. He was able to block out the gravity of the situation, narrowing his focus to the thirty feet of green he had to negotiate between the ball and the hole. His execution was flawless. "That's a feeling I'll remember for the rest of my life," he said. "It was just an unbelievable putt."

The players halved the thirty-sixth hole, sending the match into overtime. On the first extra hole, the par-4 ninth, Scott had an opportunity to stop Woods in his tracks. He had an eighteen-foot putt for birdie to win the match, and the ball rolled just over the right edge of the hole. "I put a bad stroke on it," Scott said, "and just pushed it. It was real close, but it didn't have a chance."

On the second playoff hole, the par-3 tenth, Woods hit his tee shot to within seven feet of the hole, and the pressure was again on Scott. Once more he hit his tee shot over the green into thick rough behind the hole, only a few yards from where he had chipped in for birdie on the twenty-eighth hole of the match.

"Lightning will not strike twice," Earl Woods told a man standing next to him.

Scott's chip missed the hole this time and rolled to a stop six feet away, the best he could do without hitting the pin. First to putt, Tiger lagged his birdie putt to within eighteen inches of the hole. Scott's par putt lipped out; he had failed to hit it hard enough and it tailed off, taking with it his last hope for an upset. Tiger tapped in his putt, lifted his arms in triumph, and allowed the roar of the crowd to wash over him. "It was a numbing feeling," he said later.

He then hugged his mother, who, for the first time, was on hand to watch him win an Amateur. In the two previous years, she had chosen to stay home to tend the family dogs, but she was determined to be there when her son made history. Then extending a USGA custom to its sixth year, Tiger embraced his father on the green where the winning match had ended, each of them crying unabashedly.

Scott was left to ponder what might have been if his opponent had been anyone other than Tiger Woods. His five-hole lead was not so much surrendered as it was eradicated by Woods, whose capacity to stare down and overcome adversity was already legendary. Woods shot the equivalent of a 65 in the afternoon round, and hit every green in regulation. "Given the circumstances," Tiger said, "this has got to be my best round." Neither player made a bogey from the twenty-fourth hole until the thirty-eighth.

"You figure it would be good enough," a disconsolate Scott

said of a five-hole lead. "But against Tiger Woods no lead is secure. He knows how to focus and to just put in the death blow. He knows how to attack. And he's not afraid to do it, either. He's unbelievable.

"This was probably the best Amateur match ever. Just to be a part of it was special. There were no losers today. I feel like a winner. I got my shot at him and came up a lip short. I was attempting to stop history, but I was unsuccessful. He's just so difficult to beat. He's going to give those pros all they can handle when he goes out there. I don't know how much more he has to prove around here."

Much of the golf world had been enticed to tune in to the match. Overnight ratings showed the Amateur final on NBC with more than double the audience of the World Series of Golf on CBS that same day, a tribute to Woods's talent and appeal. It was also the fourth-highest-rated Sunday golf telecast of the year behind only the Masters, the U.S. Open, and the Bob Hope Chrysler Classic.

Afterward, Earl and Kultida and Harmon's wife, Lillian, sat on a couch in the privacy of the men's locker room, each of them sifting through their emotions. "That boy never does anything easy," Earl said, between sips of a tumbler of medicinal vodka designed to bring his heart rate back to normal. "He has exercised my heart for the past six years."

The party began in earnest a short time later, in a corporate tent adjacent to the clubhouse. The sponsor, to no one's surprise, was Nike. IMG's Hughes Norton was there, as was Nike's Phil Knight, the two men responsible for charting Woods's immediate future. Later the party moved to the home where the Woodses were staying, but as celebrations go, it was subdued. In the moments following the conclusion of the match, Woods declared that he would "celebrate like hell tonight." But as the evening wound down, he quietly played cards with Byron Bell.

At a time when he should have been riding a wave of euphoria, he was anchored by the weight of a very difficult week. Energy is required to celebrate properly, and he was running on empty.

His decision to turn pro, and the frenzy that would accompany it in the next few days, tempered the celebration as well. Tiger's work, however remarkable and historical, was not over; it was in fact only beginning. At twenty years old, he had arrived at the pinnacle of amateur golf, only to discover a more prohibitive peak unfolding ahead. He had loosened Bobby Jones's stranglehold on the claim of greatest amateur golfer in history. This was an extraordinary accomplishment that, by the time the sun came up the following morning, would count for nothing in his greater quest—that represented by Jack Nicklaus and his eighteen major championships.

The journey was about to begin, and the corporate jet was standing by.

chapter twelve

After his victory in the U.S. Amateur on Sunday, Tiger longed to be able to hit the pause button on his frantic life, but instead he found himself in a fast-forward mode. When he arrived in Milwaukee on Monday afternoon, he was mentally and physically exhausted from the grueling week of golf. In seven days he had played 154 holes—most of them under intense pressure—and he had been heavily involved in completing his plans to turn professional. There was no time allotted for rest on his agenda. In two days, he would announce to the world that he was a professional golfer. Only a day later, he was scheduled to make his professional debut in the Greater Milwaukee Open.

The world at large remained unaware that Tiger intended to play Greater Milwaukee as a professional. He had decided to keep his decision to himself until the Wednesday afternoon news conference at Brown Deer Park Golf Course, the site of the tournament in Glendale, Wisconsin. Word began to leak of his impending announcement, however, and the next morning several newspapers revealed his intention to declare himself a professional that week. True to his generally reticent nature, he was relieved rather than outraged that he had not been allowed to make the announcement himself. He had intended to play as an amateur in the pro-am on Wednesday, a ruse that would have been exposed as such at the news conference later that day.

The charade officially ended on Tuesday afternoon, when Tiger released a statement to the media:

> This is to confirm that, as of now, I am a professional golfer. I will not answer any questions, or have any further comment, until tomorrow at 2:30 p.m. at my scheduled press conference.
>
> I would appreciate the media respecting my wishes to practice without distraction today. I will be available to answer your questions tomorrow.

The Greater Milwaukee Open was one of seven tournaments into which Woods had received sponsors' exemptions, the maximum allowed to those who are not yet members of the PGA Tour. He had seven tournaments in which to earn enough money to finish among the top 125 money winners, a requirement for PGA Tour membership for the following year.

The original plan was for him to play at Milwaukee and in the Quad City Classic in Coal Valley, Illinois, two weeks later as an amateur. Tiger wanted the opportunity to play in, and possibly win, a tour event that did not have a full complement of golf's elite. The idea was that, should he win one of the two, he would receive a two-year exemption onto the PGA Tour. If he failed, he would return to school at Stanford in late September.

During the summer, when he had begun to lean toward playing professionally, he had discreetly requested exemptions into five other tournaments: the Bell Canadian Open, the B.C. Open, the Buick Challenge, the Las Vegas Invitational, and the LaCantera Texas Open. He had asked tournament directors to keep the requests confidential in order to quell further talk about whether he was turning pro.

For many months agents had been speculating on Tiger's endorsement value once he finally made the leap into professional golf. Vinny Giles of Pros, Inc. suggested that Tiger had the potential to become the Michael Jordan of golf. He said that $5 million a year for five years was a reasonable expectation but added that if a huge corporate entity such as McDonald's entered the bidding, the number could escalate to $10 million. Oddly enough, this sort of public speculation was virtually in sync with the private negotiations taking place between IMG on behalf of the Woodses and select corporate monoliths. Nike proved to be the benefactor of choice, agreeing to pay Tiger $40 million over a period of five years. The contract also called for a $7.5 million signing bonus.

Phil Knight, the chief executive officer of Nike, was aware of the risk involved in investing so heavily in a young talent who had as yet proven nothing on the professional level. But given Woods's promise and startlingly high profile, the scale tipped decisively toward the gamble.

"What Michael Jordan did for basketball, Tiger absolutely can do for golf," Knight told *Golf World* magazine when questioned about the enormity of the deal. "The world has not seen anything like what he's going to do for the sport. It's almost art. I wasn't alive to see Claude Monet paint, but I am alive to see Tiger play, and that's pretty great."

IMG, meanwhile, had negotiated another contract for Woods with Titleist. He would play Titleist golf balls, wear a Titleist golf glove, and use a Titleist golf bag. For this he would be paid $3 million over three years.

The total of his pacts was $43 million, which represented a landslide victory in Woods's quest to better Nicklaus. When Nicklaus left Ohio State in 1961, he received what had been the most lucrative package in golf history. MacGregor agreed to pay him $450,000 in a five-year contract that had been negotiated, incidentally, by IMG. The pact included a $100,000 signing bonus, $100,000 in guaranteed royalties, and $50,000 a year for five years. By 1996 standards, this sum equaled roughly $498,000 a year. Tiger's average was nearly $9 million a year.

Back at the Woods camp, negotiations on a club contract with Titleist continued. Eventually he agreed to a $20 million, five-year package, which required that he play Titleist golf clubs once the company designed a suitable set for him. Until then, the Titleist contract permitted him to continue using the Mizuno irons that he had played throughout much of his amateur career. He was already playing a driver made by Cobra, a company that Titleist's parent company, American Brands, had recently purchased. And because he had always played Titleist golf balls and used Titleist golf gloves, the company was a comfortable fit for Tiger and, similarly, Tiger represented the qualities that Titleist was attempting to associate with its products.

The Titleist contract drove his endorsement portfolio up to $60 million over five years, earning him an average of $12 million a year. This placed him among the highest paid athletes in the world; prior to Tiger's having completed the Titleist deal, Forbes had ranked him twenty-sixth among the world's forty highest-paid athletes in 1996, with $800,000 in golf earnings and $8 million in endorsements. (Michael Jordan still set the standard on endorsements, having earned $40 million off the court in 1996.)

Tiger had traveled the light years between pauper and prince in a matter of hours. Suddenly he was a wealthy man, though at this point his wealth was entirely on paper. None of it was in his pocket. On Tuesday night he paid for dinner with a gift certificate that had been given to him upon his arrival in Milwaukee. On Wednesday morning, en route to the golf course, Butch Harmon asked whether Woods had his check book with him.

"What for?" Tiger said.

"Well, you've got to pay the entry fee."

"Butch, I don't have a hundred dollars."

Harmon had to loan him the money.

"I haven't seen a penny yet," Tiger said. "I haven't seen any check in the mail yet. I'm still broke."

Woods drove to the course Wednesday morning in his courtesy car. When he arrived at his locker, he discovered to his excitement that it had been supplied with three dozen Titleist Tour Balata balls and four new Titleist golf gloves.

"He was like a ten-year-old dropped into the middle of Toys "R" Us," Butch Harmon said.

Nike had shipped him dozens of shirts and pants, all of them arriving in Nike bags. "The best thing about getting all this stuff is the bags," Tiger said, expressing greater enthusiasm for the bags than he had for the multimillion-dollar contracts. "I'm serious. The Nike bags have so many pockets. They're awesome."

When Tiger arrived at Brown Deer Park Golf Course for the pro-am that morning, he was attired in Nike swooshes from head to toe, eleven of them altogether, including two on the bottom of each shoe. Earl Woods arrived with a total of ten swooshes attached to various parts of his clothing and shoes, and even Tiger's mother featured six swooshes, all on her shoes—although she declared that she would also be keeping her other pair of sneakers, which had been manufactured by Nike's chief competitor, Reebok. "They pay Tiger, they don't pay me," she said. Tiger had also discarded the lightweight Ping carrybag he had used at the Amateur. It had been replaced by a Titleist staff bag with *Tiger Woods* stitched onto it. The only remnants from his amateur past were the clubs and the tiger clubhead cover that his mother had made for his driver, stitched with Thai words that translate to, "Love from Mom."

The influx of media for the news conference where Woods would officially declare his professional status required that the throngs of photographers and reporters be relocated from the press tent to a large party tent cleared out for the occasion. Media credential requests had doubled from the previous year, attracting *People* and *Newsweek* magazines as well as reporters from the television show *Extra*.

Introduced by PGA Tour media official Wes Seeley, Tiger appeared nervous, which was out of character for a man who had spent the better part of his twenty years in the public arena. Tiger strode to the podium and, breaking into his trademark toothy grin, offered the now famous greeting: "Well, I guess, hello world."

The media's immediate reaction was that it was a clever opening line from a young man setting out to conquer the world, and yet still possessed with a charming naiveté. Then Woods read from a statement he had prepared:

> Several weeks ago I spoke with some very special people, my parents, and told them that after a frustrating and painful process, I was struggling with the decision to become a professional golfer.
>
> Then I spoke with a few very close friends, whose advice and counsel I trust and respect, and told them of my thoughts.
>
> The reactions of both my parents and friends were similar . . . they asked serious questions, offered their views, then, after heated debate, especially by my dad, told me they would fully support any decision I made.

He explained to the media how thoroughly and thoughtfully the decision had been made. He knew his golf game was ready and that it might have stagnated had he remained an amateur and collegiate golfer.

As Tiger spoke, his father sat proudly in a chair behind the podium, enjoying the day more than his son did. He, too, was a center of attention; he was the subject of numerous interviews and was unable to contain his fatherly pride during any of them. In one, he was asked what Tiger might have done if he hadn't gone into golf. "He would probably be a four-hundred-meter runner, and he'd be kicking Michael Johnson's ass," Earl said. "If you think his swing is pretty, you ought to see him run." Another time, Earl compared Tiger to a gunslinger in the wild west, "like the fastest gun in the West," he said. "On the golf course, he'll slit your throat in a heartbeat and think nothing of it. He's that cold-blooded."

Others weren't so happy with Tiger's arrival. The practice tee at virtually any PGA Tour site consists of a few stars and a host of career grinders, those attempting to earn a living, rather than construct a legacy. To them the game is hard, and they've paid their dues with sweat equity. It was inevitable that Woods would generate resentment from some of them. They included "the typical few bozos who get in trouble on pro-am day," veteran PGA Tour member Bruce Lietzke said. Otherwise, most players were very receptive. Curtis Strange agreed that the better players would openly welcome Woods aboard. Woods's presence, in conjunction with his success, would provide a boost to the PGA Tour, increasing both its exposure and the prize money, a boon to the entire membership. Yet a segment of the tour were still against him. Many felt that the money he was being paid could not be justified. The money was exceedingly high, even by golf standards, particularly for a player who had not yet even hit a shot.

The media were not among those harboring hostility for Tiger's burst onto the scene. A bottom-line business, television recognized that his appearance at an event was capable of increasing profits. When Tiger announced that he was turning pro, ESPN chose to televise the first two rounds, and tailored its air times around his tee times.

"The rating for the U.S. Amateur, the fact he could drive it to a 5.3 overnight when you've got Phil Mickelson and Greg Norman in the final group in another tournament, that's quite astonishing," said Jack Graham, golf producer for ABC Sports, which was broadcasting the final two rounds of the Greater Milwaukee Open. "I think if Tiger were to be one of the top two or three players on Sunday, it would be worth at least one more rating point."

Later that day, after the news conference, Woods signed his Nike contract, which officially made him a millionaire. Meanwhile, the media had discovered, via a news release distributed by a Nike representative, that the seemingly off-the-cuff opening remark Tiger had made to open his news conference was drawn directly from the advertising campaign the shoe company had designed for Woods. The title of the campaign: "Hello World."

Beginning with a three-page ad in the *Wall Street Journal* that cost nearly $275,000, and repeated in Nike's television spots that began the same week, the copy read:

> "I shot in the 70s when I was eight. I shot in the 60s when I was 12. I won the U.S. Junior Amateur when I was 14. I played in the Nissan Los Angeles Open when I was 16. I won the U.S. Amateur when I was 18. I played in the Masters when I was 19. I am the only man to win three consecutive U.S. Amateur titles. There are still golf courses in the United States that I cannot play because of the color of my skin. I'm told I'm not ready for you. Are you ready for me?"

The ad immediately sparked a controversy that was essentially focused on a single line: *There are still golf courses in the United States that I cannot play because of the color of my skin.* Media protests ranged from "factually incorrect" to "a tone out of character for golf in general and Woods in particular."

David Fay, the executive director of the USGA, was compelled to phone Nike to point out that in the ad Tiger is hypocritically wearing a golf shirt with the logo of Lochinvar Golf Club in Houston, Texas, an exclusive male-only club, where his teacher, Butch Harmon, is the director of golf.

Columnist James K. Glassman of the *Washington Post* phoned Nike and requested the list of courses that Woods was not entitled to play. A Nike spokesman admitted to him that no such courses exist: Woods's celebrity was his admission ticket to any golf course in the world, even the most stridently private.

Nike's defense was to suggest that the sentence should not be taken literally—that the message, implicit from its viewpoint, was that discrimination existed in clubs and within the sport, and that many clubs continue to refuse to admit African-American members.

The tone of the ad was lifted from the Nike primer on in-your-face marketing. But that tone does not play comfortably in golf, a game of gentility and sportsmanship. As Jerry Tarde wrote in *Golf Digest:* "Golf whispers. It doesn't shout."

Thus far, Woods had not shown an inclination toward assuming the role of outspoken advocate. Introducing more minorities to the game through his clinics and his celebrity, and in the process perhaps diminishing discrimination, had, however, been important causes that Woods had chosen to champion through his skills. But even Earl Woods accepted that Nike had erred on the tone. "It missed Tiger's personality to a degree," he said, "but that's understandable due to the lack of time Nike had to get to know him." The fact remained, however, that Tiger had approved the ad and defended its content.

Nike had perhaps seized on the naiveté of a young man deferring to those he considered the experts, by injecting controversy

into a burgeoning career heretofore largely devoid of controversy. And it was taken to task for doing so. The backlash included a number of club pros who severed ties with Nike and
declined to carry its products in their pro shops.

The ad disappeared quickly. Most believed that the company
recognized that it was bad for business. Nike responded by saying the campaign had run its course.

As for Woods, this initial ad campaign had been "hello world
and good-bye innocence."

In the first round the following morning, the first hole appeared to be an island surrounded by a sea of people. The audience was determined to be eyewitness to history, and lined the
hole from tee to green, 450 yards of humanity five deep. Jeff
Hart and John Elliott were playing with Woods, two unsuspecting Tour school graduates who had been caught in the
Woods stampede.

Tiger's caddie was Mike Cowan, better known as Fluff, and a
star of his own ESPN commercials. Fluff was on loan from Peter
Jacobsen, another Nike client whose recurring back problems
were keeping him at home and off the golf course. Fluff handed
Tiger his driver. Then the announcement came.

"From Orlando, Florida," the starter said to the crowd,
"making his professional debut, Tiger Woods."

Orlando? Woods had not been to Florida since he had won
the U.S. Amateur two years earlier, but IMG had deftly concluded that he needed a tax shelter. "No, I don't have a house
there yet," Woods said later. "I'm trying to get out of California
state income taxes. I've always wanted to live in Florida." Several years earlier, before he even understood what a tax shelter
was, and why he would need one, Woods had indeed stated his
intention of living in Orlando.

He strode to the tee that morning with a new address, a new

caddie, a new golf bag, two new endorsement contracts, and the same awe-inspiring swing. It had been expertly grooved to react correctly even under the most trying of circumstances. And this was certainly one: his first shot as a professional, with thousands watching. He struck the ball squarely on the clubface, a towering shot that did not spend its momentum until it had traveled 336 yards down the right side of the fairway. That shot alone was a powerful portent of what this new era in golf had in store.

By the sixth hole the crowd was giddy. He hit a drive that measured 330 yards, and then hit a 5-iron from 226 yards to twelve feet of the hole. "Pretty good, isn't he?" his playing partner, John Elliott, said to the gallery standing by the green. Woods made the eagle putt to go four-under par. He concluded his round at four-under par 67, a respectable professional debut.

"Given the circumstances and what I've had to do this week, it's a perfect start," Tiger said. "Yesterday was about as tough a day as I've had in a long time. It's been awfully hard trying to do what I need to do to get ready. What I really needed to do was play golf."

When he concluded his second round and scored under par for the second consecutive day, he took note of the leader board and discovered that he was eight shots in arrears of the lead, a fact that was also noted by Kelly Gibson, a journeyman pro.

"How's the boy wonder doing?" Gibson said, as he came off the course at the conclusion of his own round. "I'll bet he wasn't too happy a camper when he saw fourteen-under was leading. Welcome to the real world of golf."

Woods appreciated the gist of Gibson's message and the challenge it presented. "I looked at the board and I said, 'Geez, what do you have to do out here?'" he said. "It's weird. But you've got to expect it. This golf course isn't very hard."

By Saturday morning, the adrenaline on which he had been relying since winning the Amateur had run its course. Even a twenty-year-old runs low on energy, and after the whirlwind in which Woods had been caught up, he was spent. His weariness manifested itself in a golf game that had lost the edge it had steadily had for a week and a half. He concluded with a two-over par 73.

"Everything came to a climax," he said afterward, his weariness and disappointment etched on his face. "I was tired. You could see it in my game. I was sloppy. I was hoping to get through this week without that happening, the exhaustion taking over, but it came up. There's nothing you can do about it."

He had played with Bruce Lietzke, who never deviates from hitting a sweeping fade off the tee. Tiger was amused at Lietzke's ability to consistently start his tee shot at the galleries left of the fairway, sending them scurrying for cover, then carving the ball back to the middle of the fairway. For his part, Lietzke saw past Woods's errant shots to the potential that had the golf world salivating at the prospect of Tiger Woods, the professional.

"He's a great kid," Lietzke said. "I don't want to say kid. He handled himself wonderfully, even though he was struggling with his game. This twenty-year-old man really took it nice and did all the things a mature tour player would do. I think he's going to be a real good representative of our game. Lord knows we need it at the top. If he does become the next ambassador of golf, I believe the game is in real good hands."

Tiger chose to forgo his postround practice session, and returned to his hotel for a nap. He slept four hours, woke to eat dinner, then returned to bed and slept through to the following morning. Refreshed but hopelessly out of contention, he gave the multitudes a parting shot anyway. On the fourteenth hole of his final round, Tiger made a hole-in-one with a 6-iron from two-hundred-two yards, the ninth ace of his life. The crowd erupted into a sustained ovation that escorted Woods from the tee to the green.

"It was wild," he recounted in amazement. "They didn't have to do it. It was a good shot that happened to turn out perfect. I tried to punch it under the wind, but when I hit it it went higher, and I thought the wind would snag it. But it landed near the hole, and then everybody around the green was jumping up and down. People said it was a hole-in-one, and then I got excited."

Tiger shot 68 in the final round and tied for sixtieth. He earned $2,544 and had only one more obligation before he could put his first week as a professional behind him: a Monday night appearance on the ABC news show *Nightline* to talk about his achievements and his impact on the sport.

At the rain-shortened Canadian Open the following week, Woods had rounds of 70, 70, and 68, the latter equaling the low round of the final day. He finished in eleventh place, earning $37,500. During the event, he was again questioned about the propriety of the Nike ad. "Golf has been a sport where a lot of people have been denied the privilege of just playing," he said, "and it's nice to be able to get that out in the open. Let's not shun this issue anymore. It's a fact, and unfortunately I've had to experience that growing up. And I still do, but now let's talk about it, let's get it out in the open."

The third stop on his tour was the Quad City Classic, a PGA Tour outpost in Coal Valley, Illinois. Aware of what an appearance by Tiger would do for the live gate, tournament officials were euphoric when he requested a sponsor's exemption. "The phones started ringing and haven't stopped yet," Todd Nicholson, the tournament chairman, said on the eve of the tournament. "We're grinning so hard our faces hurt."

The Quad City Classic is a tournament held late in the year, off the beaten path, and it generally has difficulty finding enough recognizable names to fill its marquee and attract crowds. It had been threatened with being pushed even further into obscurity by the Presidents Cup, an event featuring a U.S. team versus an international team. The Presidents Cup—held outside Washington, D.C.—and the Quad City Classic were held concurrently, but the Presidents Cup featured golf royalty. Greg Norman, Ernie Els, and Nick Price were playing for the international team; Fred Couples, Phil Mickelson, and Tom Lehman were the core of the U.S. side.

The Quad City Classic had Tiger Woods, however, and it relied on him to trump the Presidents Cup. Tiger opened the tournament with rounds of 69 and 64, which gave him a one-stroke lead entering the weekend, piquing interest in an otherwise forgotten event. Reporters from the *New York Times*, the Associated Press, and *Sports Illustrated* began to check airline schedules in the event that they would have to abandon the Presidents Cup and head to Coal Valley, Illinois. The Quad City Classic, meanwhile, ran out of tickets and had to print more to accommodate the weekend demand.

An apocryphal story had been circulating at the Quad City Classic. It claimed that Woods had attempted to get onto a riverboat casino, despite the fact that he was underage. When he was unable to produce identification that showed he was twenty-one, the doorman refused him passage. Another man in line pointed out that this was Tiger Woods. "I don't care if he's the Lion King," the guard allegedly said. "He's still got to have a valid ID."

Other players at the tournament began referring to Tiger as the Lion King, though not to his face. It was part of the recurring resentment that his celebrity had fostered, gradually dissipating only as it became increasingly clear that he possessed the game to warrant the attention and money he was receiving.

"There's no one that's really jealous," Fred Couples explained. "To me it's kind of fun. If anybody was going to be jealous, it might be over a guy who gets $40 million and then comes out here and can't play the game of golf. This guy can obviously play, and maybe the companies signing him up are getting a helluva deal."

Tiger shot a 69 in the third round to retain his one-stroke lead, much to the PGA Tour's dismay. The Presidents Cup is a showcase event for the Tour, but with Tiger on the threshold of winning at Quad City in only his third start as a professional, a large group of reporters rushed from the Presidents Cup to the D.C. airport and boarded planes with Midwest destinations. Earl Woods, meanwhile, noted that Tiger had never lost a tournament he was leading entering the final round, and he fully expected his son to win.

The reporters who hastily evacuated the Presidents Cup could have stayed put. On the fourth hole of the final round, Woods attempted to fade his drive, but fell prey to what golfers call the double cross. He aimed left and pull-hooked his drive into a pond. He took a penalty stroke and a drop and attempted to thread his ball through a small opening in the trees. Instead, the ball hit a tree and bounced back into the pond, resulting in another penalty stroke.

Two more shots and two putts gave him a quadruple-bogey 8 that turned a three-stroke lead into a one-stroke deficit. Still, he climbed back into a tie for the lead by the seventh hole, where he four-putted the green, never to recover. "I was expecting him to win," said the winner, Ed Fiori. "It was his tournament to win. He was playing great. If he doesn't hit that bad shot he's off to the races." Fiori is the antithesis of Woods; he is short, stocky, forty-three, and a short hitter. "It was kind of like the rat snake getting the cobra," he said. Woods finished in a tie for fifth, earning $42,150.

"It's kind of hard for me to say exactly what I'm going to learn from it," Woods said later, reflecting on his loss. "I'm pretty pissed off. But I will tell you one thing: I am going to learn a lot. The way I look at it is that I broke in at Milwaukee and did okay. I did better in Canada. Today I not only broke the top ten barrier, but the top five too. So that's progress."

His collapse brought no admonishments from his parents, who had taught him that failure is an acceptable outcome, provided he make the requisite effort to learn from it, turn it around, and later succeed. "That's right," Kultida said laughing. "I tell him, 'Tiger, you play like shit, but Mom still loves you.'"

Despite his collapse at Quad City, Tiger was steadily climbing the money list. His earnings had grown to $82,194, 166th, with four events remaining. The B.C. Open in Endicott, New York, was next on his schedule, and his arrival there was trumpeted around town on newspaper vending boxes: "There's a TIGER in town!" Woods's appearance swelled the crowds, the largest in tournament history.

He shot rounds of 68, 66, and 66, tying him for third, three shots behind the leaders, heading into the final round. On a wet Sunday, Fred Funk birdied four of the first six holes to open a seven-stroke lead over Woods, when it began raining in earnest. The round was eventually canceled, and Woods finished in a tie for third, three strokes behind the winner, Funk, who was asked what Tiger needs to be successful. "A good accountant," he said smiling.

His four-week take had reached $140,194, placing him 128th on the money list, erasing any doubts about his ability to earn his PGA Tour membership. Finishing among the top 125 money winners now seemed only a formality.

When he arrived in Pine Mountain, Georgia, for the Buick Challenge a day later, he was a contented man. "This is the most relaxed I've been," he said. But after playing nine holes in a practice round on Tuesday with Davis Love III, Peter Jacobsen, and Jeff Sluman, he concluded that he needed to take time off. "He was sleepwalking the last few holes," Jacobsen said. On Wednesday morning, Tiger informed tournament officials of his intent to withdraw, that he was tired and needed a break—his first since before the U.S. Amateur.

On Thursday night he was to have been the guest of honor at a dinner where he would receive the Fred Haskins Award, college golf's equivalent of the Heisman Trophy. The dinner in Pine Mountain had been planned for several months, and by withdrawing from the event, Tiger in effect withdrew from the dinner as well. His agent, Hughes Norton, who had driven him to the airport, issued a formal statement from Tiger:

> I came here fully intending to play in the Buick Challenge. I realized last night that I was actually mentally exhausted and that if I played I would be doing a disservice to myself and those who came to watch me play. Withdrawing from a tournament is not something that I am accustomed to doing. I have expressed my apologies and my regrets to the officials of the Buick Challenge.

"It's tough for the tournament here, but withdrawing was not something he wanted to do," Norton said. "There wasn't any other choice. He's going to take three days to try and recharge his batteries and relax. In fact, I'm amazed it took this long. I thought he might hit the wall before now. I think most people would have withdrawn from B.C."

The criticism hit hard and fast, and most of it came from the locker room, where even those players who considered themselves allies were upset by Woods's actions.

Curtis Strange: "This tournament was one of the seven to help him out at the beginning when he needed help to get his card, and how quickly he forgot that. But I bet the Buicks of the world won't forget too quickly."

Davis Love III: "Everybody has been telling him how great he is. I guess he's starting to believe it."

Tom Kite: "I don't ever remember being tired when I was twenty."

Peter Jacobsen: "I feel badly for him, but he's stepped off the anonymity sidewalk. He's in the parade now. He's going to be scrutinized. One thing, you can't compare him to Nicklaus and Palmer anymore, because they never did this."

Even Arnold Palmer was critical. "Tiger should have played," he said. "He should have gone to the dinner. The lesson is you don't make commitments you can't fulfill, unless you're on your deathbed. People will forget about it in a week, but once you do what he did, the second time is probably a little easier. And you can't fall into that trap. The important thing is how he handles it from here."

Tiger was a target less for withdrawing from the tournament than for missing the Haskins dinner Thursday night. More than two hundred people had traveled to Pine Mountain, Georgia, for the affair, and the tournament sponsor had footed the bill, an outlay of about $30,000. Without Tiger in attendance, the dinner was canceled.

Tiger was stung by the breadth of the criticism, though some of the PGA Tour players responsible began contacting him with a familiar refrain: that their words had been taken out of context (even though their statements were similarly reported by several news sources in attendance). He acknowledged that he had made a mistake and sent letters of apology to each person who had been planning to attend the dinner. "I've written a letter to all the people that were going to attend the banquet, and apologized for what I did," Tiger said. "I knew what I did was wrong. I should have withdrawn from the tournament, but have gone to the banquet."

Later, he wrote a column for *Golf World* magazine, explaining his actions and apologizing further. The piece was headlined, "Learning from my mistakes."

> I am human . . . and I do make mistakes. The decision to miss the Fred Haskins Award dinner being held in my honor two weeks ago was one of them. Wow, did I get blasted for that and for withdrawing from the Buick Challenge . . . I didn't realize how tired I was after the U.S. Amateur . . . I never got a chance to rest. I kept playing . . . I didn't even think about the dinner. I realize now that what I did was wrong. But hindsight is 20-20.

Perhaps not coincidentally, the Buick Challenge was the first tournament at which Tiger had been left alone on the road in his professional career. Earl Woods had gone home to California, and Tiger's teacher, Butch Harmon, had gone home to Houston. Each of them noted on several occasions that if he had been there, this would not have happened. Earl even promised that Tiger had a commitment to make good on the money Buick had lost on the Haskins dinner canceled on Tiger's account.

Finally, Tiger was able to return to Orlando for a brief hiatus. He reappeared the following Monday in Las Vegas, where he was to play in the Las Vegas Invitational. The criticism continued to dog him, but he had discovered long ago that the best way to silence his detractors was his ace in the hole, and he went to Las Vegas determined to play it.

Let your clubs speak for you.

Tiger was not a rookie in a traditional sense, stretching dollars from one town to the next in an effort to remain solvent. He did not have to concern himself with whether his earnings kept pace with his expenses by searching for inexpensive housing, or flying coach, or, when feasible, driving from one tournament site to another.

With a superstar's bankroll, Tiger now traveled in the kind of luxury that only a fortunate few in golf know. From the moment he turned professional, he flew on chartered jets and stayed in the finest hotels. He was not playing to pay his bills, either; he was playing to win golf tournaments. The $60 million in endorsement contracts served only to simplify his quest. "I'm telling you, if somebody handed you enough money to be comfortable for the rest of your life, it would probably make a four-footer a little bit easier," PGA Championship winner Mark Brooks said, explaining how such an extravagant sum could diminish pressure. "It has nothing to do with the level of love for the game or the passion for the game. It's a pure, simple fact."

Travel is the nemesis of the professional golfer; there are virtually no such things as home games. Tiger was at least spared the inconvenience of commercial air travel, such as lost luggage, crowded terminals, and inflexible airline schedules. As a tour player, his address changed each week. "This is my house," Tiger told a *Sports Illustrated* writer who was with him in his hotel at the B.C. Open in Endicott, New York. He ran down a list of the "house's" amenities, which included maid service and elevators, then bemoaned the fact that he would be moving to another "house" the following week.

His "house" in Las Vegas, where he was playing in the Las Vegas Invitational, was in the high-rent district: a penthouse suite at the MGM Grand. It afforded him an unobstructed view of the expansive desert floor, but true to his nature, Tiger was focused only on his next meal. Early in the week he descended to the casino floor in the private elevator that serviced the penthouse and went to an ATM to fetch money for food. An inanimate device, unaware of Tiger's $60 million in endorsement contracts, the ATM knew only that he had nothing in his account, and it rejected his request. Tiger had to return to his suite and phone his mother, who was staying in a room down the hall, to ask for some money. She gave him a twenty, which he in turn gave to the butler assigned to his suite, along with instructions to retrieve a Big Mac and fries.

Another time that week, he asked his mother to iron a shirt for him. Tiger was skilled with an iron, of course, but only the kind used for propelling golf balls. He had been raised by a doting mother and domesticity was not his strong suit. At Stanford he had even taken his laundry to be done by his half sister, Royce Woods, who lived in nearby San Jose. In return, he promised to buy her a house one day.

Despite the carnival-like atmosphere of Las Vegas, Tiger had no distractions. Whether he was Tiger Woods or the Lion King, he was not old enough to gamble, and the only thing for him to do was to play golf. He also had his mother there to care for him. All the elements were in place for a breakthrough week.

For the first time in weeks, Tiger's mind was uncluttered by the business matters that had dogged him since the Amateur. The previous week, IMG had broken protocol and presented a business proposition to Tiger directly, a deal that was certain to consume significant blocks of his time. Although Tiger had seemed amenable to the deal, Earl Woods, president of ETW, Inc., was irritated. He thought the timing of the transaction may have had something to do with his absence; he was home in California at the time and had not been asked for his input. Among Earl's responsibilities as president of ETW is to act as a buffer between client and agent, a safeguard to ensure that golf remain Tiger's top priority, and that outside interests not detract from his son's ambitions. Prior to departing for Las Vegas, Tiger was assured by his father that from then on all business proposals would first go through Earl, freeing Woods's mind to focus on golf.

Earl felt that, barring distractions, Tiger would quickly win a PGA Tour event. Nearly six months earlier, he had recommended that his son enter two lesser events on the PGA Tour, "to give him a chance to win one." This was not a father's arrogance at work so much as his confidence in a son who had consistently proven that anything was possible. At the Milwaukee Open, Earl predicted that victory was imminent. "I'm not your typical optimistic parent," he said. "I'm very objective. Giving Tiger seven shots at a tournament, he's going to win one." The Monday before the Las Vegas Invitational began, Earl predicted that this was the tournament Tiger would win. He had seen Tiger improve in each week of his professional career, and it occurred to him that it was only natural that he choose an entertainment capital as the stage on which to win his first professional golf tournament.

"Remember my theory about the whole thing not being an accident, that it's being orchestrated?" Earl said. "I saw it at Quad City. I saw 'the man upstairs' present the young man with the opportunity, let him feel it. Then 'he' said, 'no.' What the 'man' said was, 'you're ready, but patience, my man.' "

A moderately strong field is attracted to the Las Vegas Invitational, which offers a large purse—$1.6 million—and the enticing extracurricular activities at the casinos. It is a five-round event played on three different golf courses, not one of which is remotely as difficult as drawing successfully to an inside straight. Low ball was the game at the Las Vegas Invitational, and when Woods opened with a 70 at the Las Vegas Country Club it appeared as though he had already removed himself from contention.

The additional round afforded by a ninety-hole event, however, provided him ample time to play his way back into contention; he began by shooting a nine-under par 63 that included twelve 3s in the second round. "He wasn't even putting that well," said his sports psychologist Jay Brunza, who was in Tiger's gallery that day. "If he'd had one of his good putting rounds, he might have shot 59 or 58."

He had gained a stroke on the lead, from eight back to seven back. He then trimmed another stroke in the third round with a 68, followed that with a 67 in the fourth, and entered the final round trailing by four.

On Sunday, Tiger opened by holing a fifteen-foot birdie putt. "This could be the day," his teacher Butch Harmon said. "His swing really looked good on the practice range. He knows he putted well yesterday and didn't make anything. This could be it."

Four hours later, he stood in the eighteenth fairway, tied for the lead, envisioning his father's stern face and hearing his voice. As he was reaching for a 9-iron, he heard his father tell him, "If you're going to take the water out of play, take the *damn* water out of play." Tiger told his caddie, Fluff, about the ingrained reminder, and both of them began chuckling. He returned the 9-iron to the bag and pulled out an 8-iron.

He made a par at eighteen to close with a 64 and was tied with Davis Love III, who was still on the course. Once Tiger had signed his scorecard, he was invited to go to the ESPN broadcast booth, but he declined. He went instead to the practice tee, to keep loose in the event of a playoff. It was a fortuitous decision. Davis Love III was unable to make birdie to win at the eighteenth hole, sending him and Tiger into a sudden-death playoff.

Tiger found the situation ironic; in a practice round only a week earlier he had mentioned to Love that he had hoped to play him head to head down the stretch of a tournament.

Love hit first in the playoff, which began at the eighteenth hole. Hitting a driver, he put his ball in the middle of the fairway. "Nice shot," Woods said, undeterred. On the tee he acted more like a confident, seasoned professional than a scared kid out of his element. He pulled a 3-wood from his bag and he, too, hit his ball down the middle, only a few yards short of Love's. This gave him a tactical advantage: the opportunity to hit first from the fairway, to return the pressure to Love. Woods hit his second shot about eighteen feet right of the pin.

"I thought it was interesting how Tiger hit a 3-wood off the tee," his former Stanford teammate Conrad Ray said, watching on television in Palo Alto, "and he was short of Davis Love's ball, so he could hit first. I would bet, in his mind, he turned that into a match-play situation. He hit 3-wood off the tee so he could hit first from the fairway and hit it to the middle of the green. And now Davis Love has a 7-iron in his hands and knows Tiger is eighteen feet from the hole for birdie."

A swing that had been sound for ninety holes suddenly accelerated, and Love came over the top on his second shot, pulling the ball toward the water. He actually struck the ball too hard, to his good fortune, and the ball cleared the hazard, but landed in a back bunker. His bunker shot went six feet past the hole, moving Woods to the threshold of winning in only his fifth event as a professional, sooner than anyone but he and his father could have reasonably expected.

Tiger lagged his birdie putt to within two feet of the hole. He tapped it in for par, leaving Love with a six-foot par putt to extend the playoff. Love missed it on the low side and Woods, in only his fifth event as a professional, in what he called one of his most memorable moments in golf, became a winner. After shaking hands with Love, a beaming Woods turned to hug his teacher, Butch Harmon, and then embraced his mother. After withdrawing from the Buick Challenge the week before, he had accepted the blame and absorbed the criticism, then responded in the way he knew best—with his clubs.

"We were all trying to prolong the inevitable," Love said. "We knew he was going to win. I just didn't want it to be today. We know how good he is. We know he's the next force on the tour, the next great player."

Disregarding his premonition about Tiger winning, Earl had chosen that week to stay at home and feed the two family dogs so that Kultida could go to see her son play. He was content to watch the tournament on television, though ESPN made the task difficult. The final round of the tournament had run long, causing a conflict with ESPN's National Football League *Prime Time* wrap-up show. The network opted to return to the studio, meanwhile promising the audience that it would not miss a single shot in the playoff.

Unfortunately for Earl, a moment that would be heralded by CNN, among others, as the best story in golf since Nicklaus won the Masters in 1986, had the drama sucked from it by ESPN's coverage decisions. It showed both Woods's and Love's approach shots, then returned to Chris Berman in the studio. By the time it returned to the golf, Tiger was putting for the championship. The station had not returned in time to show Love's bunker shot, leaving viewers, including one anxious father, without a clue as to what had transpired in the interim. When Tiger missed his putt, Love's bunker shot was shown on tape. Earl was livid at ESPN.

Monitoring their son's progress on television has been a frustrating experience at best for Earl and Kultida. The British Open telecast, for instance, ran scores continuously, scrolling the names in alphabetical order in the upper left corner of the picture, but it inadvertently omitted Woods, the last name on the scroll. It ended with Weibring, then started over, infuriating Kultida, who was home watching and unable to learn how her son was playing. Eventually she had to put in a call to Scotland in order to get an update. Moreover, the cable company that serves the Woods's neighborhood in Cypress did not offer the Golf Channel, which televised four of the tournaments in which Tiger was playing in September and October. Each day, Kultida had to drive to the home of Bryon Bell's parents, in a neighborhood that did receive the Golf Channel, so that she could watch her son play.

Since she had not seen her son since the Greater Milwaukee Open, Kultida chose to go to Las Vegas to watch him play. She too suspected that he might win there, and she was rewarded for her effort.

The week before, *Golf World* magazine had featured Woods on its cover. "HOW GOOD IS HE?" the headline asked. The following week a victorious Woods reappeared on the cover with the headline, ". . . HE'S THAT GOOD."

A few days later, a letter arrived in the mail from Raymond Floyd, who offered his "heartiest congratulations on your fantastic win."

The letter invited Tiger to come to Miami for a one-on-one short game clinic with Floyd, who is among the best around a green in golf history. Tiger, through his parents, had requested an audience with Floyd, but Floyd concluded his letter by wondering how much help Woods really needed at this point. It was frightening for many in the golf world to realize that, despite his success, Tiger was not yet nearly as good as he expected to be.

The victory at Las Vegas made his place on the money list moot; it had earned him a PGA Tour exemption for the remainder of 1996, and for 1997 and 1998 as well. He also wanted to use the victory as an opportunity to rest, but he did not want to compound the mistake he had made by withdrawing from the Buick Challenge. So he chose to honor his commitment to play in the LaCantera Texas Open, one among the seven tournaments that had graciously extended him a sponsor's invitation. With his earnings having reached $437,194, he now had an opportunity to finish among the top thirty money winners, which would earn him passage into the season finale, the lucrative Tour Championship. To enhance his chances, he also entered the Walt Disney World/Oldsmobile Classic the week after the Texas Open.

At Texas, Tiger was again in contention, though a third-round 73 put him seven shots back of the leader. That night, seated courtside at the San Antonio Spurs game at the Alamodome, he considered the number he would be required to shoot to win the tournament. He came up with 64.

The next day, after fifteen holes, Woods was one down to David Ogrin. But he missed a five-foot birdie putt to tie at the sixteenth hole, and he missed the green with his tee shot at seventeen, resulting in a bogey that ended his bid. A third-place check for $81,600 did not console him. "The idea is to go out and win the damn thing," he said. He shot 67 and lost by two. A 64 would have given him a one-stroke victory.

The Walt Disney World/Oldsmobile Classic was played in Woods's new hometown of Orlando. He was home but not necessarily comfortable. His agent, Hughes Norton, apparently had passed on a virus to Earl when they had played a round of golf. Earl was now stricken with bronchitis, and Tiger had caught a cold.

"Don't put a needle in my head," Woods said to those inquiring about his health on the eve of the tournament. "It might burst. I've got a sore throat. I'm totally congested. I'm dizzy. Other than that, I feel fine."

His golf game, at least, was healthy. He opened the tournament with a 69, a respectable number that nevertheless left him six shots behind the leaders. "Pop," Woods said firmly to his father that night, "I'm going to shoot 63 tomorrow and get back into this tournament."

Earl thought that establishing a target score applied undue pressure, but he opted to say nothing to his son, who had an early tee time the following morning. When Tiger returned to the house at the end of his round, Earl was just getting out of bed.

"What did you shoot?" he asked.

"Sixty-three," Tiger replied nonchalantly.

He followed that with a 69 that put him within a shot of the leaders. Prior to the final round, Woods's mother phoned and reminded him to wear red, his lucky color, according to his birth month, December. She noted that he had worn red in the U.S. Amateur final and won, and that he had worn blue the previous week in San Antonio and lost. Mother knows best, and on Sunday Woods donned a red shirt with the ubiquitous Nike swoosh, and a red hat with a black bill.

In the final round, Tiger was paired with Payne Stewart, which gave him an opportunity to test his skill down the stretch against an established star, a former winner of the U.S. Open and the PGA Championship. The gallery was uncharacteristically large, which made moving around somewhat difficult. When the players were on the sixth green, vast numbers of people moved toward the seventh tee by cutting through some brush and, in the process, started a chain reaction. Their movements inadvertently spooked a deer, which fled in the direction of a pond and attracted the attention of a hungry alligator. The gator climbed the bank of the pond and made an unsuccessful swipe at dinner as it darted past.

In the midst of this wild animal kingdom, and in the shadow of Disney's Magic Kingdom, Stewart and Tiger engaged in generational warfare, the thirty-nine-year-old former Open champion versus the precocious twenty-year-old who had single-handedly moved golf into the mainstream sports world. Was it possible that he would win again, for the second time in three weeks?

Stewart, determined to squelch that suggestion, shot a 67, but it was not good enough. Tiger shot a 66 and finished seventy-two holes one stroke ahead of Stewart. "All the accolades need to go to Tiger for the way he's played and conducted himself over the last eight weeks," Stewart said at the end of the tournament. "He's the shot in the arm our tour needed."

Tiger, however, was only the leader in the clubhouse; Taylor Smith was still on the course with an opportunity to tie him. And he did so when he birdied the eighteenth hole. But earlier in his round, Smith's playing partner, Lennie Clements, noticed that Smith had been using a putter with an illegal grip and reported the infraction to PGA Tour officials. The violation had been inadvertent, but Smith was still disqualified. He chose to play out his round anyway, then pleaded his case to Tour officials, to no avail. Woods had won for the second time in three weeks, though he would have preferred winning in a playoff.

"It's very gratifying, very satisfying," he said, "but I have some mixed feelings about it. I feel like there should have been a playoff with Taylor. He birdied eighteen to get into it. I've never had anything like that happen to me, and I've never heard of anything like it."

The victory increased Tiger's winnings to $734,790, pushing him to twenty-third on the money list and earning him passage into the Tour Championship the following week in Tulsa, Oklahoma. The inevitable comparisons began anew. Woods finished in the top ten in five of his first seven professional tournaments, winning two of them; Nicklaus finished in the top ten only once in his first seven, and failed to win any of them.

Tiger's entrance into the world of professional golf ranks among the greatest debuts in history, and it was the best stretch of golf on the PGA Tour in fourteen years. In his five previous tournaments, Woods had finished fifth, third, first, third, and fifth to become the first player to finish in the top five in five straight tournaments since Curtis Strange had done so in 1982. Of Woods's last twenty-one rounds, he had shot in the 60s in eighteen of them, including eleven of the last twelve.

"It may be surprising to some, but it's not surprising to people who know me," he said, "but I haven't really played my best yet. I've hit the ball pretty good, but not the greatest. I haven't had the greatest putting round yet. I've had two four-putts, many three-putts, and in Canada I hit four water balls. I've been in a whole lot of trees where I had to pitch out. Really, my game has been really good or kind of bad. I've been too aggressive on some three-putts, or put myself in bad places because of such bad iron shots. There's room for improvement in every facet of my game."

His words hinted at perceived failure, but in fact he had been overwhelmingly successful and had accomplished his immediate goal—to earn his PGA Tour membership for 1997. "Everything else I've accomplished is a bonus," he said. "My initial goal was to get out here and have a place to play next year. And I accomplished that. And then I kind of went beyond that to where now I'm exempt for two years."

Each year the top thirty money winners qualify for the Tour Championship, and the fact that Woods was among them proved Curtis Strange prophetic. Back at Milwaukee, Strange had said that the moment Woods became a PGA Tour member he'd be a top thirty player, with the potential to be the best in the world. He had debuted at thirty-seventh in the world on the Sony Ranking, the fastest ascension in the history of the charts. A strong field at Tulsa at the end of October would provide a test to see whether Tiger was already one of the two or three best players in the world.

His ascension piqued the interest of mainstream television, and interviews began piling up, including one with ABC's *World News Tonight,* which had made Woods its person of the week. In a two-month span, Tiger had taken golf out of sports and onto network news. He was now assigned guards as a buffer between himself and the crowds; he had had four at Disney and one at Tulsa. Virtually anywhere in the country, he now had trouble dining out without attracting attention. "It's like he's the pope," Kultida said.

In the first round of the Tour Championship, Brad Faxon was playing with the person of the week, and the galleries were so vast that they were actually of benefit to the players. "There are so many people, they frame the hole for you," said Faxon, who shot a two-under par 68. "They give you definition, where you want to hit the ball."

Tiger opened with an even-par 70, a nondescript round framed by bogeys on the first and eighteenth holes. It was only the seventh time in twenty-eight professional rounds that he had failed to break 70. Still, he was tied for eighth, four strokes off the lead.

It would be as close as he got to contending. At 2 A.M. Friday Earl began having chest pains. He woke Kultida in their Tulsa hotel room and asked that she get him to the hospital. She called the paramedics, who arrived moments later and took him to Saint Francis Hospital near the hotel.

Earl had had a quadruple bypass a decade earlier, but it had not moved him to give up his cigarette and red meat habits. Now he was having a mild heart attack, "a warning from 'the man upstairs,' " as he put it a few weeks later. He was admitted to the Trauma Emergency Center at Saint Francis Hospital at 2:51 A.M.

Kultida called Tiger in his room to tell him of his father's condition but advised him to stay in bed and sleep. Tiger, however, was frantic at this recurrence of his father's heart problems and went to the hospital anyway. He stayed until five A.M. before returning to his hotel in a pointless attempt to get a few more hours of sleep.

When he teed off that morning, he was there in body only. His mind was with his father who, unbeknownst to Tiger, was resting comfortably and watching the golf tournament on television. Tiger was on the third hole when Kultida arrived at the course. She came, she said, to reassure Tiger, through her presence, that Earl's condition was stable. "If he sees me here, he'll know he's doing okay," she said. If he had not seen her he might have assumed the worst.

At the twelfth hole, as he made his way down the fairway, Tiger spotted his mother in the gallery.

"Mom, any more reports on Dad?" he yelled over.

"He's okay," she said. "I'm here."

"But he doesn't believe Mom," she said a moment later. "He needs to see for himself. His concentration is not there."

That was evident. He was unable to focus on golf and shot an eight-over par 78. He could have withdrawn and no one would have objected, but he played because his father wanted him to play. "I didn't want to be here today," he said at the end of his round, "because there are more important things in life than golf. I love my dad to death, and I wouldn't want to see anything happen to him."

Tiger's relationship with his father had always been void of the Richter Scale activity that most fathers and sons encounter during the teen years. The first time he overindulged at a fraternity party, Tiger got sick and humbly told the story to his father. Rather than getting angry, Earl told him he could maintain control by drinking spacers of water or soda between beers. This was the kind of interaction the two shared, and it explains Tiger's respectful, mature behavior even as a kid.

Every time he was honored—whether in front of a ballroom full of people as he received the 1993 Dial Award as the nation's best high school athlete, or at the podium for the 1994 Espy Awards, televised by ESPN—he announced to the world that his father was his best friend. Earl was forty-three when Tiger was born and, as a result, theirs is a relationship more like that common between a grandfather and his grandson. "Our relationship is based on friendship and mutual respect," Earl Woods said.

When Tiger was fourteen, an age when most kids perceive their parents as enemies of sorts, he called his father "the coolest guy I know."

Though his relationship with his mother is often overlooked because Earl has more often accompanied him around the country, Tiger enjoys a bond with her that is also exceptionally strong. When she is at home and he is playing in a tournament on the road, he phones home virtually every day to keep her apprised of how he is playing.

But his father has been his soul mate, the man who not only taught him to play, but also taught him lessons about life— about the importance of honoring his heritage and about his responsibility to give back to the game. He was perhaps the only idol Tiger had ever had. He may have outgrown his dependence on his father as a provider of moral support, but playing while Earl was in a hospital bed with tubes attached to him was not the way it was supposed to be as Tiger set out to conquer the world.

Earl had had a heavy cigarette habit, and his son had resigned himself to the fact that he was incapable of convincing his father to stop smoking. Only a few weeks earlier, a phone call to Tiger's hotel room at the Quad City Classic had found him alone.

"Where's your dad?" the caller asked.

"He's up in room 513," Woods said. "In the smoking section."

Now his father was in a hospital room, and although Tiger played on, the momentum he had established by winning at Disney had dissipated in the early hours of the morning, when Earl's chest pains began. After his round later that day, he anxiously hurried over to the hospital to confirm that his father's condition was as stable as his mother had said. Earl was alert and complaining about his confinement, a sign that instantly relieved Tiger; he knew that his father was recovering. This was further indicated when Earl stated that he intended to have a cigarette the moment he was released from the hospital. Given what he had put everyone through, even this retired Green Beret was inadequately armed to resist the battalion of doctors, wife, son, and friends who vehemently vetoed the cigarette idea.

Reassured that his father was recovering, Tiger played better in the final two rounds, shooting a 72 and a 68. He finished in a tie for twenty-first, concluding his initial foray onto the PGA Tour. In only eight events, he had earned $790,594 and was twenty-fourth on the money list.

The Woodses had planned to return home to Orange County via a commercial airline on a route that included a change of planes and a long layover. Tiger insisted that they return via charter jet, the first time he found himself caring for his parents.

He was also taking more responsibility for his own actions. In attempting to rectify the mistake he had made by forcing the cancellation of the Haskins Award dinner, he had requested that the dinner be rescheduled. He was presented with a variety of options, but decided that returning to Pine Mountain, Georgia, to receive the award was the best way.

Tiger and his father flew into Pine Mountain on a Monday afternoon, November 12. Later that night Tiger stood in front of the audience that had assembled five weeks later than scheduled, and apologized. "My actions were wrong," he said. "I'm sorry for any inconvenience I may have caused. I'll never make that mistake again."

The media criticism of Tiger diminished in the aftermath of the apology. Jack Nicklaus even recalled that he had similarly erred when he was a nineteen-year-old amateur playing in the PGA Tour's Azalea Open the week prior to the Masters. Through thirty-six holes, he was in fourteenth place, but he decided that the two rounds he had played were preparation enough for the Masters. So he withdrew. "I was a kid," Nicklaus told *Senior Golfer* magazine, "and Ed Carter and Joe Black showed up as soon as I got to the Masters. They said, 'Jack, you can't do that on Tour.' I haven't done it since. We all go through things we wish we hadn't done. I don't think you'll see Tiger do that again."

From Pine Mountain, Tiger flew to Portland, Oregon, to select a wardrobe from Nike, which had recently announced its intention of designing a Tiger Woods line of golf attire. Earl went along as Tiger's unofficial wardrobe consultant. As an amateur, Tiger often wore Earl's shirts because of the extra room they afforded him; now Earl wanted to ensure that when he wore Tiger's shirts he would be stylish. The pair then returned to Cypress, California, Tiger's first trip home since leaving for the U.S. Amateur nearly three months earlier.

When he entered the house, he was happily reunited with the two family dogs, particularly Joey, who often slept on his bed in his absence. Joey had a habit of picking up windfall avocados from the yard, bringing them through the doggy door, and eating them on Tiger's bed, leaving the mess and the pit behind. It was only a minor nuisance for Tiger, who found the cramped bedroom considerably more comfortable than any penthouse suite.

Tiger was supposed to have played in the Shark Shootout that week in Westlake Village, California. The Shark Shootout is an event operated by the International Management Group, but hosted by Greg Norman, a former IMG client who had defected a few years earlier. When Tiger outlined his fall schedule in Milwaukee, he had included the Shark Shootout in his initial plans. But in the weeks to follow, representatives of Norman said that Woods had not been invited. Eventually Tiger concluded that he'd rather not go where he wasn't wanted, and planned instead to go to the Australian Open the following week.

Eventually, an official invitation was extended to Tiger to compete in the Shark Shootout, but he declined, citing his full schedule. He took that week off, then left for Australia, where he was reportedly receiving an appearance fee of $195,000, considerably more than Australia's own, Greg Norman, was reported to be receiving.

Advance ticket sales for the Australian Open were four times greater than they'd been the year before, illustrating Tiger's growing international appeal. The people had come to see better golf than Woods produced in the first round, when he shot a 79, twelve shots behind the leader, Norman. Tiger recovered, however, finishing with rounds of 72, 71, and 70, and tying for fifth in his first international appearance as a professional. Still, he bemoaned his play. "I could not get anything positive going," he said. "Physically and mentally I made a lot of mistakes and when you do that, you usually don't win. I spent most of the time in bed, trying to recover from a cold. It was just a tough week."

He returned to the States shortly after to participate in the Skins Game, an event to which only established stars are usually invited. In midsummer, Barry Frank, an IMG executive and Skins Game official, said that the Skins Game lineup would not be announced until after the U.S. Amateur. Frank had said that he wanted to keep options open in the event Woods turned pro, in which case he would be invited to play.

The Skins Game was a second-season event that had grown increasingly stale in recent years. The prize money, $540,000, was no longer substantial by professional golf standards, and once Nicklaus and Palmer had graduated to the Senior Skins, they took much of the appeal with them. The television ratings for the event had steadily declined.

Tiger's appearance reenergized the Skins Game, as media from around the world descended on the Southern California desert to cover what had often been decried as a made-for-television event. They were there to cover one player.

"There's only a handful of golfers in the world that are significant ratings boosters," tournament director Chuck Gerber said. "Tiger's obviously one of them." ABC Sports, which was televising the Skins Game, promoted the event by interviewing Woods at halftime on its *Monday Night Football* telecast.

The Skins Game had moved to a new course, Rancho La Quinta Country Club, which was more forgiving of errant tee shots than the site of the four previous Skins Games, in Palm Desert. The standard format is that, on each hole, the players play for a designated amount of money—in this instance, the first six holes were worth $20,000 each; the second six $30,000 each; and the final six $40,000 each If no one wins a hole outright, the money carries over to the following hole.

Anticipating that Woods and John Daly would engage in an informal long-drive contest, the Skins Game committee decided to install large yardage markers alongside each fairway and visible from the blimp overhead. In this way, they provided viewers the opportunity to gauge the lengths of the drives for themselves.

From the first hole, Woods and Daly began to flex their muscles, Daly hitting his drive 340 yards, Woods hitting his 318. At the wide-open, par-5 seventeenth hole, each of them caught their drives flush. Woods's drive measured 321 yards, Daly's 320. In the end they concluded that their long-drive contest had been a draw.

Fred Couples won the event, earning $280,000, but was reduced to third billing behind Woods and Daly. Woods finished third with $40,000.

Attracting a greater audience that day than even the Notre Dame-USC football game, the Skins Game had an overnight rating of 8.2, the largest in its history and among the highest-rated golf telecasts ever. The year before, the telecast had generated an overnight rating of only 4.4.

"There's not a question that Tiger Woods's emergence on our tour has created the interest," Tom Watson said. "It's great. This shows the golf world that they want to see him. The sport is better for it."

It was the latest installment of the Tigermania that was sweeping the golf world. It was most evident in the large number of kids who tailed him throughout his golf tournaments. They leaned against the gallery ropes, attempting to catch a glimpse of him, and they stalked him between rounds in search of autographs. At the Scottish Open the previous summer, Woods emerged from the scorer's tent and encountered more than a hundred kids, each of them clamoring to acquire his signature.

Exasperated, Tiger finally yelled, "Stop!"

He then pulled the smallest boy from the crowd and instructed the others to line up behind him. "No one gets an auto-graph unless you do," he said.

On Halloween one boy about ten years old came to the home of an editor at *Senior Golfer* magazine. He wore a Tiger Woods costume: a short-sleeved golf shirt and sweater vest, and a cap with the Nike swoosh and the bill rounded into an arc, in the style of his hero. He also carried a small golf bag in which he was collecting his candy.

After the Skins Game, in the midst of the Tiger madness, Earl Woods's doctor phoned him and complained that Tiger had cost him a thousand dollars.

"Why?" Earl asked.

"I took my son to the Skins Game and he was so enamored with Tiger," the doctor replied. "I've been trying to get him out on the golf course for years, and he's always been in a hurry to go home. Yesterday I couldn't drag him away from the driving range. All he talks about is golf and Tiger. All he wants for Christmas are golf clubs."

Tigermania is likely to penetrate deepest into minority communities, introducing a game once considered foreign, the private domain of the white upper class. But its influence on kids will be no less substantial.

"I thought if I kept progressing in golf and I came on the Tour and did really well, I could help golf, bring more minorities into the game, and make it more diverse," Woods said. "I thought that would be my biggest impact. But the impact on the kids is something I love to do. I love doing clinics. I love helping them out."

Indeed, he has a pied piper quality; children of every race and background tail him, for he is closer to them in age than their parents are. "They can relate to me," Tiger said. "I'm not far from being a teenager myself. When people yell, 'You the man,' I always say, 'Not legally.' "

Tiger, in turn, has always responded to kids. At the 1994 U.S. Amateur in Ponte Vedra, Florida, a twelve-year-old boy, J. B. Berka of Jacksonville, was the standard-bearer for each of Woods's matches, and Woods befriended him and dubbed him his good luck charm. When Woods made his Masters debut the following spring, he invited Berka and his father, Dick, to Augusta and provided them with tickets to a practice round.

"Of course he's going to have an impact," said Watson Dobbs, a PGA of America pro at Westchester Golf Course near Los Angeles International Airport. Dobbs is among an alarmingly small number of black club pros in the country. "All the kids want to emulate him. He's a hero, period. He's like Michael Jordan to them. They all want to be like him. They want to swing like him. They want to play like him."

Tiger is determined to respond in kind, by continuing to conduct clinics on his travels. When he formed his corporation, one of the first priorities was to establish a Tiger Woods Foundation to conduct his clinics and other charitable endeavors, each of them geared toward youth. "Giving Back Love," became the theme of his foundation.

Nike recognized Tiger's following among kids and structured its second Woods ad accordingly. In it, a number of kids are shown playing golf, with the words, "I am Tiger Woods," superimposed.

But Tiger's appeal is not limited to youth. In only eight weeks as a professional golfer, he had installed himself as golf's leading marquee attraction, apparent by his visibility on the news rack. When he won the Walt Disney World/Oldsmobile Classic, he was featured on the covers of *Sports Illustrated* and *Golf World* and was already on the covers of *Golf Digest* and *Golf* magazines. In the last five months of 1996, he appeared on covers of *Golf World* five times, *Golf Digest* once, *Golf* once, *Newsweek* once, and *Sports Illustrated* twice.

Traits not ordinarily associated with golf—youth and diversity—were among the instruments of Tigermania, and from the rubble of these shattered stereotypes, a new era in golf had emerged in time to escort the game into the next millennium.

But Tiger, underscoring the youth element of the equation, was not looking ahead to the twenty-first century. He was looking forward only to his twenty-first birthday.

Tiger Woods is poised between adolescence and adulthood, a charming place where corporate responsibilities and Big Mac attacks are woven into the fabric of a day. He will gleefully show off the Mickey Mouse watch he was given for winning the Walt Disney World/Oldsmobile Classic, but the $216,000 he also received will barely evoke a yawn.

At the Tour Championship in Tulsa in October 1996, he was giddy at having the opportunity to drive a Mercedes-Benz, one of a fleet used as courtesy cars for the thirty players. He also discovered that a Mercedes fit into the drive-through lane at a fast-food restaurant as comfortably as did his old Toyota Supra.

"Then why don't you buy a Mercedes," Butch Harmon suggested.

"Do you know how much one of these costs?" Tiger said, ending the discussion.

"He's cheap," Earl Woods said later.

Cheap, as in he never had money of his own and is uncertain what to do with it now that he has it?

"No, he's cheap, period," Earl said, laughing.

Frugality did not prevent Woods from spending a half-million dollars on a townhouse in the exclusive Isleworth community in Orlando, however. The townhouse is adjacent to the driving range, which explains his willingness to approve the expenditure. For Tiger, living next to a driving range is the equivalent of a child living next to a playground. He spent another $250,000 to have the home decorated. Why, the thrifty Woods wondered in the process, do two pillows cost six hundred dollars?

He has his own golf cart at Isleworth, and the feature he is most proud of is its compact disc player, on which he plays what Harmon calls "god-awful music." Woods's preferences run from rap to R&B to a particular favorite that is without a genre, ESPN's Jock Jams.

Every six months Titleist provides him two thousand Titleist Tour Balata golf balls, 100 compression, to practice with. When Tiger hits them onto the range at Isleworth, they are collected with the other range balls, then separated, bagged up, and placed on his front porch. When it is time for lunch and for practice, he phones over to the club and places an order. He then grabs a bag of balls from his porch, motors over to the range in his golf cart, and his lunch is waiting for him.

This is Tiger's Nirvana.

When he moved in, he quickly met most of the other kids in the neighborhood, including Ken Griffey Jr., a winter resident who has become a close friend. When Tiger went to Ponte Vedra to meet with PGA Tour Commissioner Tim Finchem in November, Griffey and Mark McGwire took a helicopter over to join Woods in a friendly game on the TPC Stadium Course at Sawgrass.

Tiger often golfs with another Isleworth neighbor, Mark O'Meara, or hangs out with Anfernee Hardaway of the Orlando Magic. Wesley Snipes is a neighbor as well.

A boyish charm, parlayed with a multimillion-dollar golf swing and a multiethnic heritage, has constructed for him a future that apparently knows no bounds. Tom Watson has called him the most important man to come into the game in fifty years. John Merchant, the founder of the National Minority Golf Foundation, is reluctant to diminish the contributions Arnold Palmer has made, but he will say that Woods is potentially one of the two or three most important men ever to come into the game.

"I think his impact, assuming he realizes anywhere close to his potential, will be the same as Palmer or Nicklaus, and maybe more," Merchant said.

Representatives of a PGA Tour event contacted Merchant about having Woods conduct a junior clinic the Tuesday of tournament week, and dubbing it Tiger Tuesday. They assured Merchant that they could produce twenty-five hundred kids. "And somewhere between thirty and sixty percent of them will be minorities," Merchant said. "If he were to spend an hour doing a clinic and five minutes talking to them and twenty minutes signing autographs, each one of those kids is going to go home talking about Tiger Woods. And maybe picking up a golf club. He brings attention to the game, some awareness of it. He brings credibility to it. It's okay to play golf. His commitment, as I believe it exists, is to open the game up and to increase involvement of minorities in golf. He's going to spend time at this.

"My secretary handed me a fax that talks about an event in Virginia, that if Tiger got involved it could raise twenty-five to fifty thousand dollars for charity. It's an invitation from the Chamber of Commerce of a major Southern city. When was the last time the Chamber of Commerce had anything to do with a black man? It's amazing."

The galleries following Woods are a rich mix of race and age and gender. He not only appeals to kids; he is an adult attraction as well. On Sunday at the Las Vegas Invitational, Davis Love III said, "We had forty people walking with us, and I knew twenty of them. I think Tiger got about seventy-five percent of the crowd, Fred Couples got twenty percent, and we got the other five percent; and we were playing in the final group."

He has already become the celebrity celebrities want to

know. Don King invited him to attend the Mike Tyson-Evander Holyfield fight in Las Vegas in November 1996. Kevin Costner agreed to be his partner at the AT&T Pebble Beach National Pro-Am. Michael Jordan, a Nike teammate, also wants to play golf with him.

"I truly have so much admiration for this kid," Jordan said. "He's one of my idols now, and he's twenty. I'm really in awe of him." Is Woods potentially the Michael Jordan of golf? "The similarities between he and I, that's just a standard of measurement for things ahead for him, as it was for me when I was coming out, with Dr. J," Jordan said.

It became immediately apparent that Tiger's name on the marquee ensured a tournament success, as the Skins Game on Thanksgiving Day weekend demonstrated. "I think we're looking at the next major superstar in golf," said Don Ohlmeyer, who had conceived the idea of the Skins Game. "Tiger has a flair for the dramatic and one of those smiles that lights up the screen."

The smile is only one element in an expressive package capable of infusing golf with charisma. His passion and Technicolor persona also include the occasional blue streak triggered by a misguided golf shot. "He's pure excitement on the golf course," Stanford teammate Jake Poe said. "For a game that sometimes people don't consider exciting, he is going to change that. He's going to redefine the game. He already has."

"Every week, thousands of people who don't even play golf are following him," Butch Harmon said. "They might decide to play golf now. Tiger is the brightest thing to come along in who knows how long. And that's really the bottom line. It's not just good for Tiger. It's good for everyone."

It is particularly good for Tiger, however. He is already a cottage industry that will eventually grow into a conglomerate. From the moment he first put a tee in the ground as a professional, he was playing only for trophies; the prize money was inconsequential to his net worth, which, with $60 million in endorsement contracts, was already substantial.

In Europe and Asia, he will command appearance fees that will teeter only between a fortune and a small fortune, excluding prize money. He reportedly received $195,000 for playing in the Australian Open, a sum he agreed to before becoming a winner on the PGA Tour. As his success grows, so will his appearance fees.

His Thai heritage strategically positions him to tap into the growing Asian golf market. "His future in the Pacific rim is enormous," John Merchant said, "when you look at what might happen with the growth in those countries because of Tiger. Nobody out there can spur growth like he can."

Yet it is not about money, Earl Woods insists. It is about competing and winning. Prior to earning his PGA Tour membership, Tiger began considering what it would take for him to earn a place on the U.S. Ryder Cup team in 1997. He concluded that a few victories in 1997 ought to be sufficient. "He thinks about winning and nothing else," Davis Love III said. "He's not playing for the money. I like the way he thinks."

He will grow to appreciate the money, certainly, but however affluent he is, money is not likely to smother his desire to continuously challenge himself to improve. His only concern is whether he has the wherewithal in his pocket to eat at McDonald's; when he does, Tiger is content.

"A hundred dollars is a lot of money to him," his father said.

In fact the money that has meant the most to Woods was the $2,544 he earned in his professional debut at the Greater Milwaukee Open. "This is my money," he says. "I earned it." And the other, the $60 million? "I didn't earn that," he says shrugging.

But he is earning it every day. "He's going to be one of those guys who can push product," Curtis Strange said. Each day at the U.S. Amateur, Woods wore a black cap with a U.S. Amateur logo, and the bill bent into an arc. Television viewers took notice and began phoning Pumpkin Ridge, placing orders for the caps. The club sold out of them days before the tournament had concluded. Now Tiger wears hats bearing the Nike swoosh, as do the countless kids in the galleries of the tournaments he is playing.

After Tiger won two of the first seven tournaments he played as a professional, the thought occurred to Earl that Nike CEO Phil Knight probably considered the $40 million outlay a bargain. "I told him this, right to his face," Earl said grinning, "just wait until next time." Next time, when his five-year contract with Nike has expired, Tiger will have an established track record, both as a golfer and as a corporate spokesman. If he plays to a level remotely commensurate with his potential, the Michael Jordan of golf will have emerged.

Yet the Woods family is not intent on chasing the dollar at the expense of Tiger's development as a golfer. The first two employees hired by Woods's corporation were his mother and father, who are there to ensure that he not lose sight of his objective. Earl and Kultida insist that he proceed cautiously, especially since the lucrative Nike and Titleist contracts allow him to be more selective in evaluating other endorsement opportunities. They only represent a beginning. Eventually, Tiger is almost certain to surpass Jack Nicklaus and Arnold Palmer in annual endorsement earnings. Late in 1996, Pepsi inquired about hiring Tiger as a corporate spokesman. He discussed the opportunity with his parents, who advised against it. "We're not greedy," Earl said. "Time is more important to him." Professional golf was uncharted territory for Tiger, who found it imperative that he learn to manage his time before assuming additional corporate responsibilities.

Once he has established the amount of time and energy he is able to devote to business ventures, his endorsement portfolio is certain to expand. Given his appetite for burgers and fries, he is a natural fit for a fast-food chain. Automobile manufacturers and golfers have a long history, too.

Woods, in turn, is capable of paying dividends in a variety of ways. "I've been at several tournaments he's played," PGA Tour commissioner Tim Finchem said, "and we see a lot of kids, a lot of minorities in the gallery, a lot of enthusiasm. Our sponsors report that he drives more ticket sales, which will turn out more charitable dollars. During the first network event he was on, the ratings went up. He's a plus all around. There's a very positive feeling about the young man. He creates positive feelings and that's good. His performance is incredible and that in and of itself is a story, even if you didn't have all the other things going on about his age, his ancestry. He can have a profound impact on the depth and texture of the sport over the long term, if he continues to play at this level."

Performance is the engine driving his burgeoning business empire and philanthropic endeavors, and his limitless potential as a golfer is the element that has the golf world salivating over the possibilities. Hours after Woods had won his second U.S. Amateur Championship, the euphoria, perhaps in concert with the free-flowing celebratory champagne, moved Earl Woods to conclude that Tiger might eventually win fourteen major championships. A few days after Tiger won his third U.S. Amateur Championship, Johnny Miller trumped Earl. "With his distance and his technique," Miller wrote in *Golf World*, "Tiger may win fifteen majors. He may well be classified in the same breath as Nicklaus when he's done."

When, in a five-week stretch, Tiger finished fifth, third, first, third, and first, it had become apparent that however excessive these predictions may at first have appeared, they no longer seemed out of the realm of possibility. It is also possible that Woods's expectations for himself far exceed winning fourteen or fifteen major championships. At this point, who could argue that they are unattainable?

"I heard Nicklaus say that Tiger ought to win at least ten Masters," PGA Championship winner Mark Brooks said. "He could. He could win twenty-five Masters. He could win every Masters he plays the rest of his life. It's unlikely. The scariest thing is somebody overheard somebody in the locker room saying he hasn't even shot his A game yet. If he's got an A game that he hasn't shown yet, then we're probably all in trouble."

He produced his A game only once in 1996, Tiger said, when he shot rounds of 61 and 65 on the first day of the Pacific 10 Championships, eighteen-under par, giving him a fourteen-stroke lead. "That was the last time I played really well," he said at the conclusion of the Australian Open. "I have not reached that level as a pro yet."

Tiger no doubt intends to continue his pursuit of perfection, sometimes turning down unique opportunities that come his way. Among the calls he received in the aftermath of his victory in the U.S. Amateur was one from the Sultan of Brunei, the richest man in the world. He invited Woods to come to Brunei to play golf with him. Woods declined. He hadn't the time. To this day, his focus remains on his golf career, for ultimately his celebrity will ring hollow unless his production on the golf course keeps pace.

It is a tall order. The specter of burnout is real given the degree to which he has pursued the game in his twenty-one years, but then that does not account for the fire smoldering within. Golf is not only his sport, but also his vice—he is addicted to the game; his appetite for it is insatiable.

When he is home, he often has a golf club in his hands, his L wedge or his putter, and he is incessantly working on his chipping or his putting stroke. "He'd rather golf than eat, and he's certainly a professional eater," Earl Woods told *Newsweek* magazine. "He'd rather golf than sleep, and he's a professional sleeper."

Moreover Tiger has learned a simple device as a hedge against burnout. His father taught him to listen to his body, and when his body informs him that a respite is in order, he puts away his clubs.

The fire within, the defense mechanism against burnout, manifested itself in anger at the Quad City Classic, his third tournament as a professional. Tiger had a three-stroke lead early in the final round, when he hit his tee shot into a pond. He took a drop and attempted an imprudent recovery shot through an opening in the trees. He missed and his ball struck a tree and returned to the water. At that point Woods took the offending club, a 6-iron, and began chopping at a tree, as though he was attempting to bring it down. An ax might have worked better, but that would be missing the point. Immortality is constructed not with lumber, but with passion.

If Tiger is destined to become the greatest player in history, it is because in his mind anything less is unacceptable.

* * *

Virtually from the moment he turned professional, Tiger began building the case that he was already the greatest player in the world. He had won two of his first seven PGA Tour events, and at the PGA Tour Awards Dinner following the second round of the Mercedes Championship at La Costa in January, he was named the 1996 Tour rookie of the year.

"Wow," Tiger said emphatically upon receiving the award, using a word that the golf world would be repeating two days later in tribute. In a sudden-death playoff with Tour player of the year Tom Lehman, Woods nearly made a hole-in-one, his ball stopping only six inches from the hole, and for the third time in nine Tour events, he was a winner.

This victory earned him a new automobile and $216,000 in gas money to fuel an imposing journey for which no map is available, inasmuch as only Nicklaus has ever made the trek. Then again, no map is necessary. Tiger is guided by his obsession. "I'm getting paid a lot to do something that I love to do," he said. "It's like a drug. If I don't have it, I go crazy. Sometimes I lie in bed for hours just thinking about a shot or my round. Golf is something that is always on my mind."

His restlessness is the byproduct of a confident man who is eager for a new day to begin. Twenty-one years into his life, he has already had what is tantamount to a productive career. But even in the dead of night, Tiger is not inclined to rest on his laurels, for he understands that as good as yesterday might have been for him, tomorrow promises to be even better.